New Directions for
Community Colleges

Arthur M. Cohen
EDITOR-IN-CHIEF

Caroline Q. Durdella
Nathan R. Durdella
ASSOCIATE EDITORS

Amy Fara Edwards
MANAGING EDITOR

Global Development of the Community College Model

Carmen L. McCrink
Heidi Whitford
Natasha C. Stubbs

EDITORS

Number 177 • Spring 2017
Jossey-Bass
San Francisco

Global Development of the Community College Model
Carmen L. McCrink, Heidi Whitford, Natasha C. Stubbs (eds.)
New Directions for Community Colleges, no. 177

Editor-in-Chief: *Arthur M. Cohen*
Associate Editors: *Caroline Q. Durdella, Nathan R. Durdella*
Managing Editor: *Amy Fara Edwards*

New Directions for Community Colleges, (ISSN 0194-3081; Online ISSN: 1536-0733), is published quarterly by Wiley Subscription Services, Inc., a Wiley Company, 111 River St., Hoboken, NJ 07030-5774 USA.

Postmaster: Send all address changes to *New Directions for Community Colleges*, John Wiley & Sons Inc., C/O The Sheridan Press, PO Box 465, Hanover, PA 17331 USA.

Information for subscribers
New Directions for Community Colleges is published in 4 issues per year. Institutional subscription prices for 2017 are:
Print & Online: US$454 (US), US$507 (Canada & Mexico), US$554 (Rest of World), €363 (Europe), £285 (UK). Prices are exclusive of tax. Asia-Pacific GST, Canadian GST/HST and European VAT will be applied at the appropriate rates. For more information on current tax rates, please go to www.wileyonlinelibrary.com/tax-vat. The price includes online access to the current and all online backfiles to January 1st 2013, where available. For other pricing options, including access information and terms and conditions, please visit www.wileyonlinelibrary.com/access.

Delivery Terms and Legal Title
Where the subscription price includes print issues and delivery is to the recipient's address, delivery terms are **Delivered at Place** (DAP); the recipient is responsible for paying any import duty or taxes. Title to all issues transfers FOB our shipping point, freight prepaid. We will endeavour to fulfil claims for missing or damaged copies within six months of publication, within our reasonable discretion and subject to availability.

Back issues: Single issues from current and recent volumes are available at the current single issue price from cs-journals@wiley.com.

Publisher: New Directions for Community Colleges is published by Wiley Periodicals, Inc., 350 Main St., Malden, MA 02148–5020.

Journal Customer Services: For ordering information, claims and any enquiry concerning your journal subscription please go to www.wileycustomerhelp.com/ask or contact your nearest office.
Americas: Email: cs-journals@wiley.com; Tel: +1 781 388 8598 or +1 800 835 6770 (toll free in the USA & Canada).
Europe, Middle East and Africa: Email: cs-journals@wiley.com; Tel: +44 (0) 1865 778315.
Asia Pacific: Email: cs-journals@wiley.com; Tel: +65 6511 8000.
Japan: For Japanese speaking support, Email: cs-japan@wiley.com.
Visit our Online Customer Help available in 7 languages at www.wileycustomerhelp.com/ask

Production Editor: Shreya Srivastava (email: shsrivsata@wiley.com).

Wiley's Corporate Citizenship initiative seeks to address the environmental, social, economic, and ethical challenges faced in our business and which are important to our diverse stakeholder groups. Since launching the initiative, we have focused on sharing our content with those in need, enhancing community philanthropy, reducing our carbon impact, creating global guidelines and best practices for paper use, establishing a vendor code of ethics, and engaging our colleagues and other stakeholders in our efforts. Follow our progress at www.wiley.com/go/citizenship

View this journal online at wileyonlinelibrary.com/journal/cc

Wiley is a founding member of the UN-backed HINARI, AGORA, and OARE initiatives. They are now collectively known as Research4Life, making online scientific content available free or at nominal cost to researchers in developing countries. Please visit Wiley's Content Access – Corporate Citizenship site: http://www.wiley.com/WileyCDA/Section/id-390082.html

Printed in the USA by The Sheridan Group.

Address for Editorial Correspondence should be sent to the Editor-in-Chief, Arthur M. Cohen, at 1749 Mandeville Lane, Los Angeles, CA 90049. All manuscripts receive anonymous reviews by external referees.

Abstracting and Indexing Services
The Journal is indexed by Academic Search Alumni Edition (EBSCO Publishing); Education Index/Abstracts (EBSCO Publishing); ERA: Educational Research Abstracts Online (T&F); ERIC: Educational Resources Information Center (CSC); MLA International Bibliography (MLA).

Cover design: Wiley
Cover Images: © Lava 4 images | Shutterstock

For submission instructions, subscription and all other information visit:
wileyonlinelibrary.com/journal/cc

CONTENTS

EDITORS' NOTES

The concept of community colleges has existed for more than a century in United States. The mission of these institutions is centered on access to postsecondary education that focuses on the needs of the community in which they are located. The opportunities available include general education coursework leading to an associate of arts degree, vocational training that culminates with an associate of science degree, and continuing education. For a high percentage of students entering the community college system, the ability to transfer credits to a university and obtain a baccalaureate degree serves as a motivating factor and the fulfillment of the promise for equality through access to a higher education. The success of this model has garnered international attention from countries such as Canada, Chile, China, South Korea, India, South Africa, Turkey, and New Zealand, to name a few. The need for a highly skilled and well-educated workforce is a common theme. Additionally, the internationalization of community colleges in United States, through the expansion of academic programs, continues to gain momentum.

Within the context of North America, the United States and Canada are highlighted in this volume. In Chapter 1, Chase-Mayoral suggests the need for institutions founded on the educational, economic, and social needs of a community to also consider how the spirit of educational entrepreneurialism plays a role. She hypothesizes that this concept is a prerequisite for a community to develop the idea of establishing and sustaining these types of institutions. Furthering this idea, Sianos discusses why Ontario's *Differentiation Policy Framework for Postsecondary Education* was developed and its impact on Ontario's postsecondary system. This framework was designed as a response to the need for a highly skilled workforce; however, it is believed that this system encourages elitist reform. The focus of Chapter 3 is South America. Through the lens of organizational learning theory, McCrink and Whitford describe the outcomes of a partnership between a community college in the United States and a university in Chile to develop a community college system in Chile.

Chapters 4 through 6 focus on the continent of Asia, specifically China, South Korea, and India. The development of community college-like institutions in China began as recently as the 1980s. Zhang posits identity, applicability, structure, and global impact as challenges these institutions are experiencing. Kim and Yun explore persistence within 2-year colleges as it relates to career decision making self-efficacy, academic satisfaction, and

New Directions for Community Colleges, no. 177, Spring 2017 © 2017 Wiley Periodicals, Inc.
Published online in Wiley Online Library (wileyonlinelibrary.com) • DOI: 10.1002/cc.20236

institutional support of South Korean students. The voluntary nature of enrollment within these institutions and nonexistent time limits for degree completion create an interesting context for this study. In Chapter 6, Gross examines the future direction of community colleges in India in relation to its impact on policy and procedure.

In South Africa, comprehensive universities are akin to the community college concept referenced in the United States. Wilson and Van Alebeek explore the implications of the dissolution of apartheid within the community college setting, specifically related to access, persistence, affordability, accreditation, and transfer. Similarly, in Chapter 8, Raby, Friedel, and Valeau conduct a comparative study of the completion agenda of community colleges in the United States and their global counterparts.

Chapter 9 focuses on the expansion of postsecondary education throughout the world as a means of developing individuals for a global society that is rapidly changing, technologically driven, and economically interdependent. Likewise, Tyndorf and Glass argue the necessity of 2-year and 4-year institutions as a means of increasing human capital and therefore promoting the economic growth of developing countries.

A workforce that is able to meet the needs of the local community is a priority not only for the United States but also for countries around the globe. Developing partnerships to expand academic programs is one of many alternatives for creating opportunity. Collectively, the chapters in this volume highlight the growth of the community college model inclusive of the successes and challenges that accompany change. Continued opportunities to engage in this dialogue facilitate the global expansion and development of the community college model around the world.

Carmen L. McCrink
Heidi Whitford
Natasha C. Stubbs
Editors

CARMEN L. MCCRINK is associate professor and chair of the Higher Education Administration Department at Barry University, Miami Shores, Florida.

Heidi Whitford is an assistant professor in the Higher Education Administration Department at Barry University, Miami Shores, Florida.

Natasha C. Stubbs is a doctoral candidate in the PhD in the Leadership and Education program with a specialization in higher education administration at Barry University, Miami Shores, Florida.

NEW DIRECTIONS FOR COMMUNITY COLLEGES • DOI: 10.1002/cc

1

This chapter explores the theoretical and conceptual history of the global rise of the U.S. community college model, focusing on the common missing ingredient that remains elusive among the increasing numbers of these community-based institutions.

The Global Rise of the U.S. Community College Model

Audree M. Chase-Mayoral

Making an invaluable contribution to the U.S. higher education system for more than 100 years, community colleges are in many ways its underappreciated segment. Educating close to half of the entire undergraduate student population in the United States, community colleges enroll 7.4 million credit students and 5 million noncredit students. Historically playing such a strong role within the educational system, these institutions were destined to receive attention from the international community. Thus, for at least 40 of those 100 years, American community colleges have been playing a unique role within the global higher education community. Since the formation of the Community Colleges for International Development (CCID) organization in 1981, more than 50% of the nation's 1,200 community colleges have been involved with international expansion. How and why do U.S. community colleges continue to encourage and promote the development of institutions that address the educational, vocational, and lifelong learning needs of communities worldwide? U.S. community colleges serve as a model for 2-year institutions that have rapidly changed the international educational landscape. As American community colleges respond to the needs of their local communities, so do their international counterparts. Interestingly, a minimal amount of data exists regarding what preexisting conditions are necessary in order to establish an institution of higher education that resembles a traditional community college. This chapter attempts to address this conundrum.

Conversely, as prevalent as the spread of the community college model is worldwide, several countries have not adopted this model within their educational system. While continuing to explore the increasing relevance of the expansion of community college-like institutions, conducting

NEW DIRECTIONS FOR COMMUNITY COLLEGES, no. 177, Spring 2017 © 2017 Wiley Periodicals, Inc.
Published online in Wiley Online Library (wileyonlinelibrary.com) • DOI: 10.1002/cc.20237

research on countries where the model has not yet expanded is equally as pertinent.

Present in nearly every country are federally funded organizations that support the advancement of its citizenry. For example, ministries or departments of education exist to provide primary through tertiary education, even if there are only one or two institutions of higher education in an entire country. Additionally, the existence of a ministry of labor (or equivalent thereof) would support the establishment of business and industry to support economic stability and growth. However, a nation may be lacking in both financial and human capital resources and therefore unable to address the more complex needs, such as vocational education and training, of traditionally underserved or underprivileged citizens. In cases of countries and communities with unique challenges that necessitate the improvement of socioeconomic conditions, situational factors of each of these types of communities suggest the need for an institution akin to a community college to support human capital, social capital, and economic growth.

The social capital that a community-based tertiary institution provides to a society cannot be underestimated. According to Coleman (1988), although social capital is perhaps an underanalyzed concept, it nonetheless provides evidence that combining organizational resources of a society in meaningful ways creates an organization of value to a community to further develop human capital. The necessity of building both social and human capital exists, in varying degrees, within every community around the world. Therefore, the need to provide a relevant and contextualized educational institution exists in every community around the world. In this capacity, the community college model fills a unique educational void that contributes to the investment in and development of both social and human capital in communities in the United States and worldwide.

Theoretical Framework

Supporting the notion that the U.S. community college model bridges the gap in other countries between higher education and entrance into the workforce, Steiner-Khamsi (2004) asserts that the comparative educational theory of educational borrowing posits that educational systems possess an innate need to "impart an understanding of what can be learned and imported from elsewhere (borrowing)" (p. 2). Examining the global rise of the community college model through the lens of educational borrowing builds on past concepts by stating that America's community colleges, charged with responding to local concerns that are increasingly global in nature, are uniquely positioned to play a critical part in the worldwide economic, social, and educational spheres (Treat & Hagedorn, 2013). This is not to say that community colleges in the United States are obligated to play a significant role in the development of tertiary institutions with similar missions; however, the comprehensive nature of the services they provide to other communities is logically replicable on the global scale. Additionally, research about the global rise of the traditionally American community college model supports the theory that flows exist between countries from which community college institutional counterparts develop and spread (Raby & Valeau, 2012).

The increase in community college-like institutions in other nations speaks to how the 2-year model is transported or transplanted from one context to another. But does this mean that the process of "borrowing" is selective by design or is it incorporating the entire American community college concept? The basic mission and purpose of an American community college, and indeed its moniker, strongly suggest that the "borrowing" process by each community college-like institution is selective by design and highly responsive to the local needs of each geographic context. Or perhaps an argument can be made that the spread of the community college model, whether from the North American context outward or through different flows—for example, north and south flows (Raby and Valeau, 2012), should be examined from a different perspective—that of mass institutionalized components of ways in which primary and secondary educational institutions proliferate worldwide. Normally applied to the K–12 educational environment, the same idea of mass education worldwide holds true for the replication of community-based tertiary education institutions because the basic structure, standards, and expectations are common despite uncommon and diverse socioeconomic systems and geographical contexts (Wiseman, 2014).

Much discourse is available both confirming and disputing the scope of the impact that specifically the American community college model has had on the modeling of similar institutions worldwide (Elsner, Boggs, & Irwin, 2008; Raby & Valeau, 2009; Romano, 2002; Wiseman, Chase-Mayoral, Janis, & Sachdev, 2012). Also widely noted is the acknowledgment that more in-depth research needs to occur with regard to how specifically these institutions develop in other nations (Raby & Valeau, 2009). However, notably missing in the dialogue is a discussion about how the spirit of entrepreneurialism represents a common denominator in the establishment of any institution driven by the educational, economic, and social needs of communities worldwide.

Historical Perspective

In addition to detailing the full history of the U.S. community college movement, Vaughan (2006) postulates that the sustained success of American community colleges hinges on the fact that even while landscapes develop and change, their essential mission and purpose of offering open access to higher education that is affordable, no matter the fluctuations in any economy, remain the same. Furthermore, these institutions are able to morph and change the myriad educational programs they provide not only to individual students but also to entire communities, while not compromising their core mission and dedication to teaching (Vaughan, 2006). The developing landscapes are the literal variations of cultural, economic, and social situations in more than 75 countries where community college models exist with myriad institutional names (Raby & Valeau, 2009). For more than a century, it remains undisputed that the American community college represents an integral part of higher education within the United States, even though their true impact may not have always been acknowledged as such. Four-year colleges and research universities have often been considered superior to community colleges (Dougherty, 1987). Nevertheless, increasingly social scientists are acknowledging that 2-year institutions represent a desirable choice for undergraduate students' first 2 years of tertiary education (Christensen, Baumann, Ruggles, & Sadtler, 2006). Although America's community colleges are arguably not the only forces in the development of their global institutional counterparts, the transfer component to a 4-year institution is a unique aspect of their mission that is transferrable to other global contexts.

Globally, CCID continues its work during the past 40 years to promote international partnerships between American community colleges and like institutions worldwide. The focus of these partnerships promotes primarily economic development, driven by the forces of globalization. The impact of globalization should not be underestimated when examining the spread of institutionalized education at the 2-year level. According to Holland (2010), with regard to international development studies, interaction among external and local forces has the power to establish new institutions. This assertion supports the widely held notion that the external forces of a more established community college system (whether American or not) functions in tandem with situations and needs in contextualized geographic locations to address local and community-based issues.

Coupled with the notion that external forces comingle with localized specific needs, Steiner-Khamsi (2004) asserts that studies on the effects of globalization factors on education must not only affirm the relationships between increased international exchanges of goods but must also confirm the transnational changes in national education systems. Numerous theoretical frameworks contribute to the institutionalist approach in sociology of how and why educational models spread worldwide and how they are both global and local at the same time (Meyer, 1980; Meyer, Boli, Thomas, & Ramirez, 1997; Meyer, Ramirez, & Soysal, 1992; Wiseman et al., 2012). This viewpoint further supports the notion that the establishment of a community college-like institution anywhere in the world represents a special mixture or combination of ingredients. Traditionally, these basic ingredients are financial resources, responding to the specific educational needs of the communities they serve, and adapting to the needs of business and industry (Culpepper & Thelen, 2008). However, throughout the prevailing discourse surrounding the spread of the community college model, something less tangible is missing from the formula. The variety of countries and cultural contexts that have adopted this model from America (or elsewhere) represents a unique mix of characteristics. It is difficult, in other words, to find specific preexisting conditions in every geographical location where community college-like institutions are located. Although they all theoretically have the identical mission or purpose, their structures vary considerably. However, there might be one preexisting commonality that contributes to every scenario—the presence of an educational entrepreneurial spirit within each society that establishes a community-based higher education institution.

The Missing Ingredient

Although challenging to quantify or qualify the contribution of an entrepreneurial spirit within an entire country's educational system or any given local community in which the need for innovative higher educational solutions exists, a comparative imperative exists (Wiseman & Chase-Mayoral, 2013) to search for the missing ingredient in the community college expansion formula. Community college scholars have a collective knowledge of the history of the American community college movement and its purpose and they know that this movement has expanded to other countries exponentially. In other words, they know what they know. Scholars do not know what the exact preexisting conditions are that make conditions viable to establish a community college-like institution within differing global contexts. They know that some aspects of the American model are retained and some are not. Bradach (2003) captures this concept in rephrasing Weick's (1976) theory of loosely coupled systems. When discussing replicating social and educational programs to scale, an organization might discover that only a piece of a program needs replicating, not the entire program or organization (Bradach, 2003). Thus, like K–12 educational systems in the study of mass institutionalization worldwide, this concept is also applicable to the global expansion of the traditionally American community college model. Therefore, they know what they do not know. In other words, community college scholars know that only pieces of any community college model are used in each geographical context. However, what community college scholars do not know at all is the piece of the puzzle that exists in all fledgling community colleges, irrespective of geographical or cultural contexts. The spirit of educational entrepreneurialism is that missing ingredient.

Educational entrepreneurialism involves disruption within an existing system. It involves risk-taking and innovation, as does any entrepreneurial venture. Social and educational entrepreneurs do more with less, they take calculated risks while seeking to provide real improvements to their stakeholders, and they tackle underlying causes of social and educational issues, as opposed to merely addressing symptoms of problems (Dees, 2001).

According to Wiseman (2014), one approach to explaining educational entrepreneurship is from a comparative and international education perspective and incorporates the following three components: internationalization, entrepreneurial spirit, and innovative ideas. Furthermore, according to Wiseman, "educational innovations are new or hybrid combinations of existing elements, but are often not wholly new" (p. 13). Again, this reflects the theoretical concept of educational borrowing combined with loose coupling, with the added component of an entrepreneurial spirit. When examining the global rise of the community college model, local educational and workforce training needs in every geographical context drive the innovation necessary to conceive a higher education institution that is equipped to meet these complex and diverse needs. Business and industry must constantly innovate, because of globalization and the necessity of responding to local economic needs of their communities. By definition, community colleges (and by extension, their global counterparts) perform the same function of responding to localized economic and social needs as major parts of their mission. Educational needs in the 2-year tertiary realm remain somewhat constant: to provide higher education approximating the first 2 years of a 4-year college academic program, to provide some measure of workforce training, and to provide continuing education. So in that sense, loose coupling exists in that the basic academic purpose of a 2-year institution remains essentially the same worldwide, whereas programs to address the specialized workforce needs of each localized community evolve and change to adapt to each geographical context. However, the key to jump-starting any of this is for a community—any community—to acknowledge publicly and purposefully the need for social and educational change.

For countries with educational and social challenges, Christensen's and Bower's (Christensen et al., 2006) method referred to as "catalytic innovation" suggests a sustainable process to improve conditions by establishing contextually appropriate solutions to combat social issues more effectively. These catalytic innovations represent smaller "disruptive innovations" and are identified by attempting to effect positive social change on a national scale (Christensen et al., 2006). Contributing to this need for social change, researching the need for and ultimately establishing a community college-like institution in a new country involves innovation and a disruption within a traditional country-specific context. For example, a country accustomed to a more traditional higher educational system may feel threatened by the fact that community colleges typically offer advanced-level courses without the excessive salaries of faculty who are more research oriented. Instead, they often rely on faculty with specific business and industry expertise to ensure that course curricula accurately reflect current demands of the local workforce. The idea of using instructors from business and industry is highly transferrable, no matter what area of the world, as industry experts in all facets of business communities worldwide teach in community college-like institutions. The concept of using local industry experts is disruptive to many systems of higher education globally, as they are likely to be more traditional in their approach to employing primarily research-driven faculty. The educational entrepreneurial spirit of community-based institutions fills educational gaps and encourages innovation. As Wiseman (2014) states that mass K–12 public education presents opportunities for the implementation of innovations, the same is true, if not more so, for community-based educational entrepreneurship improving ways in which tertiary education "facilitates labor market participation through employability" (p. 17). Social and educational entrepreneurship clearly plays important roles in the establishment of any community college-like institution in any part of the world.

Conclusion

Perhaps it is time to shift the discourse of how and why the U.S./North American community college model has risen so prevalently throughout the world. Scholars should conduct more research to determine how a social and educational entrepreneurial spirit must first be present in a community in order to germinate the seed of establishing and sustaining such an institution, irrespective of its moniker and socioeconomic or geographical context. Perhaps the dialogue should be how the community college movement became so scalable, sustainable, and marketable to so many parts of the world. The query of the lack of community college-like institutions in certain countries of the world presents an interesting topic for further research. Possibly, countries that lack a sense of an entrepreneurial spirit are less likely to establish community colleges. Collection of data to substantiate this hypothesis, however, presents daunting challenges, as the definition of the existence of a collective educational entrepreneurial spirit within a geographical context represents an ambiguous concept. Nonetheless, uncovering this information may provide an additional piece of the puzzle of what community college scholars do not know.

Missing in this article is the acknowledgment that resources are necessary to establish any educational institution; however, with educational entrepreneurial innovations, Wiseman (2014) postulates that "anything that can be commodified can also be established as a resource for entrepreneurship" (p. 21). American community colleges are accustomed to this concept of being adaptable, flexible, and using resources, both financial and human capital, in creative ways in order to respond to the ever-changing educational, social, economic, and cultural needs of the students and communities that they serve. How the elusive concept of an educational entrepreneurial spirit represents the missing ingredient that explains the global rise of the community college movement requires more research. The spirit of educational, and even social, entrepreneurialism runs strong in the history of the American community college movement and it continues to be replicated and reflected within its global counterparts.

References

Bradach, J. L. (2003, Spring). Going to scale: The challenge of replicating social programs. *Stanford Social Innovation Review*. Retrieved from http://www.ssireview.org/articles/entry/going_to_scale/

Christensen, C. M., Baumann, H., Ruggles, R., & Sadtler, T. M. (2006). Disruptive innovation for social change. *Harvard Business Review, 84*, 94–101.

Coleman, J. S. (1988). Social capital in the creation of human capital. *American Journal of Sociology, 94*, 95–120.

Culpepper, P. D., & Thelen, K. (2008). Institutions and collective actors in the provision of training: Historical and cross-national comparisons. In K. U. Mayer & H. Solga (Eds.), *Skill formation: Interdisciplinary and cross-national perspectives* (pp. 21–49). New York, NY: Cambridge University Press.

Dees, J. G. (2001). The meaning of "social entrepreneurship." Duke University innovation and entrepreneurship newsletter. Retrieved from https://entrepreneurship.duke.edu/news-item/the-meaning-of-social-entrepreneurship/

Dougherty, K. (1987). The effects of community colleges: Aid or hindrance to socioeconomic attainment? *Sociology of Education, 60*, 86–122.

Elsner, P., Boggs, G., & Irwin, J., (Eds.). (2008). *Global development of community colleges, technical colleges, and further education programs*. Washington, DC: Rowan & Littlefield Publishers.

Holland, D. G. (2010). Waves of educational model production: The case of higher education institutionalization in Malawi, 1964–2004. *Comparative Education Review, 54*(2), 199–222.

Meyer, J. W. (1980). The world polity and the authority of the nation-states. In A. Bergesen (Ed.), *Studies of the modern world-system*. New York, NY: Academic Press.

Meyer, J. W., Boli, J., Thomas, G. M., & Ramirez, F. O. (1997). World society and the nation-state. *American Journal of Sociology, 103*(1), 144–181.

Meyer, J. W., Ramirez, F. O., & Soysal, Y. N. (1992). World expansion of mass education, 1970–1980. *Sociology of Education, 65*(2), 128–149.

Raby, R. L., & Valeau, E. J. (Eds.). (2009). *Community college models: Globalization and higher education reform*. Dordrecht, Netherlands: Springer.

Raby, R. L., & Valeau, E. J. (2012). Educational borrowing and the emergence of community college global counterparts. In A. Wiseman, A. Chase-Mayoral, T. Janis, & A. Sachdev (Eds.), *Community colleges worldwide: Investigating the global phenomenon. International Perspectives on Education and Society Series, 17* (pp. 19–46). Bingley, UK: Emerald Group Publishing Limited.

Romano, R. (Ed.). (2002). *Internationalizing the community college*. Washington, DC: Community College Press.

Steiner-Khamsi, G. (Ed.). (2004). *The global politics of educational borrowing and lending*. New York, NY: Teachers College Press.

Treat, T., & Hagedorn, L. S. (2013). Resituating the community college in a global context. In T. Treat & L. S. Hagedorn (Eds.), *New Directions for Community Colleges: No. 161. The community college in a global context* (pp. 5–9). San Francisco, CA: Jossey-Bass.

Vaughan, G. (2006). *The community college story* (3rd ed.). Washington, DC: American Association of Community Colleges.

Weick, K. E. (1976). Educational organizations as loosely coupled systems. *Administrative Science Quarterly, 21*(1), 1–19.

Wiseman, A. (2014). Internationally comparative approaches to innovation and entrepreneurship in education. In A. Wiseman (Ed.), *International education and public sector entrepreneurship: International Perspectives on Education and Society Series, 23* (pp. 3–31). Bingley, United Kingdom: Emerald Group Publishing Limited.

Wiseman, A., & Chase-Mayoral, A. (2013). Shifting the discourse on neo-institutional theory in comparative and international education. In A. Wiseman & E. Anderson (Eds.), *Annual review of comparative and international education: International Perspectives on Education and Society Series, 20.* (pp. 99–126). Bingley, United Kingdom: Emerald Group Publishing Limited.

Wiseman, A., Chase-Mayoral, A., Janis, T., & Sachdev, A. (Eds.), (2012). Community colleges: Where are they (not)? In A. Wiseman, A. Chase-Mayoral, T. Janis, & A. Sachdev (Eds.), *Community colleges worldwide: Investigating the global phenomenon: International Perspectives on Education and Society Series, 17* (pp. 3–18). Bingley, United Kingdom: Emerald Group Publishing Limited.

AUDREE M. CHASE-MAYORAL, EdD candidate in educational leadership, is the associate director of the Office of Global Online Graduate Degrees and Training at Lehigh University's College of Education, Bethlehem, PA.

NEW DIRECTIONS FOR COMMUNITY COLLEGES • DOI: 10.1002/cc

2

The Ontario Ministry of Training, Colleges and Universities in Canada released Ontario's Differentiation Policy Framework for Postsecondary Education in 2013. This chapter examines the mandate as it pertains to the college sector.

Early Days for the Differentiation Policy Framework in Ontario

Helen Sianos

The Ontario Ministry of Training, Colleges and Universities (OMTCU) released *Ontario's Differentiation Policy Framework for Postsecondary Education*, in 2013. This framework arose as a response to the 2008 global economic downturn along with decreased levels in future enrollments for Ontario postsecondary institutions. Because of these pressures, the government stated that provincial postsecondary institutions needed to respond to these changes in order to protect and ensure their continued growth (OMTCU, 2013). The framework outlined the need for an educated, creative, knowledgeable, and skilled workforce in order to increase the international competitive advantage of the province and the quality of life for its citizens. George Brown College (2014), Seneca College (2014), and Humber College (2014) provide a snapshot of how they interpreted the framework and their response to it with the publication of their Strategic Mandate Agreements (SMAs). The collection and organization of the public data available on these three colleges reveal that they are mass-universal comprehensive institutions with elite program characteristics providing democratic access for all who wish to attend (Trow, 1973, 2005). This chapter argues that the push from the Ontario government for a highly skilled workforce educated by a formalized, institutionally differentiated postsecondary college system will create *elitist reform* (Trow, 1973, p. 30); inaccessible, *specialized* knowledge; creativity; and vocational silos in the provincial college system. The theory of differentiation versus the application of differentiation may not be as noble or productive for those seeking to attend these differentiated institutions outlined in the framework.

The first section of the chapter explains the reason for selecting the topic by providing a brief history of colleges in Ontario. The second section

NEW DIRECTIONS FOR COMMUNITY COLLEGES, no. 177, Spring 2017 © 2017 Wiley Periodicals, Inc.
Published online in Wiley Online Library (wileyonlinelibrary.com) • DOI: 10.1002/cc.20238

presents the definitions and concepts surrounding the terms *differentiation* and *diversity* from the academic writings of Huisman et al. (1995), Clark (1983), Birnbaum (1983), and Teichler (2008). These definitions are applied in the context of the colleges and the framework. Within the same section, Trow's (1973) seminal work on the transitional phases of higher education and his 21st century reflections on his original work (Trow, 2005) are discussed to frame the comparative historical and theoretical context and direction of the framework. In the third section, an examination of how differentiation and diversity were used in the framework and what they mean in the Ontario college context. The application of differentiation and diversity in *Ontario's Differentiation Policy Framework for Postsecondary Education* (OMTCU, 2013) is conceptualized within the context of Trow's theory and his "typology" (1973, p. 27), which suggests that the creation of elitist reform institutions hinders universal, democratic access. The fourth section of the chapter outlines the methods used to collect and present the comparative data about the types of credentials and programs that George Brown, Humber, and Seneca offer. The data paint a picture of three colleges that are simultaneously homogeneous (Clark, Moran, Skolnik, & Trick, 2009), differentiated (externally and vertically) (Birnbaum, 1983; van Vught, 2008), and diverse (internally by programs and types of awards granted) (Birnbaum, 1983; van Vught, 2008). The final section of the chapter postulates the findings from the data and how the three postsecondary institutions interpret the mission and mandate of the framework in their SMAs and what the road ahead looks like for these colleges.

Historical Context

In the mid-1960s, then Minister of Education, William G. Davis, introduced a bill to the Ontario Legislature for the creation of the Colleges of Applied Arts and Technology (CAATs) (Ontario Department of Education, 1967). The aim of these institutions was "the introduction of a new level and type of education...to provide through education and training, not only an equality of opportunity to all sectors of our population, but the fullest possible development of each individual to the limit of his ability" (Ontario Department of Education, 1967, p.5). The colleges would fulfill the geographic regional needs of the communities they resided in and provide another route to postsecondary education with a vocational mandate (Ontario Department of Education). Furthermore, the CAATs were "composite or comprehensive institutions...providing a wide variety of programs of varying length...the emphasis not only could but should vary from one community to another, as local needs dictate" (pp. 12–13). Davis created a system that provided democratic, regional access to postsecondary education for all in the province of Ontario to fill future vocational knowledge gaps and careers not be met by the universities (Ontario Department of Education).

The following is an abridged CAATs timeline presenting the concerns surrounding the purpose of the colleges in Ontario. Starting in 1978, approximately a little over a decade since Davis announced the creation of the CAATs, Kymlicka (1978) noted economic and demographic changes in Ontario were "likely to generate increased uncertainty with respect to the aims and responsibility of postsecondary education" (p. 102). Then, 25 years after the creation of the CAATs, Dennison and Gallagher (1986) questioned the future mandates and mission of the colleges because of the continuing changes in economics and population demographics. The historical legacy of politics, economics, and demographic trends, nearly 50 years later, were again the main concerns and reasons articulated in and for *Ontario's Differentiation Policy Framework for Postsecondary Education* (OMTCU, 2013) in the following way:

> With institutions' costs outpacing growth in revenues from operating grants and tuition, existing cost structures are under pressure. Measures that help to mitigate these pressures are needed in order to ensure the continued sustainability of our postsecondary education system. (p. 5)

The framework proceeded to explain that because of the reciprocal nature between higher education and the provincial economy, postsecondary differentiation was a means by which to sustain this government–education relationship.

Definitions and Theoretical Context

Before any discussions on the arguments for or against differentiation, definitions of diversity and differentiation are required to understand what they mean when referred to in the framework and applied to the Ontario college system.

Differentiation. Huisman et al. (1995) conceptualized and contextualized higher education differentiation from a biological perspective whereby differentiation "refers to the emergence of several parts out of a formerly integrated whole...from an integrated whole, different parts emerge, which have their specific function in relation to the other parts and the whole" (Huisman et.al., 1995, pp. 13–14). This differentiation from an "integrated whole" (p. 14) happened in Ontario in the early years of the 21st century (Clark et al., 2009; Fallis, 2013); the Ontario government created deliberate differentiation by conferring the status of Institute of Technology and Advanced Learning (ITAL) on 5 of the 24 colleges in Ontario (Clark et al., 2009). From those initial five colleges, three of them are under consideration in this chapter (Clark et al., 2009). These ITALs have their own specific functions that relate to and are part of the Ontario-wide binary college and university system (Fallis, 2013). The ITAL designation permits these colleges "to offer up to 15 per cent of their programming in bachelor's

New Directions for Community Colleges • DOI: 10.1002/cc

degree programs (the limit for other colleges is 5 per cent)" (Fallis, 2013, p. 29). The Ontario definition of differentiation, as understood and applied from Huisman's (1995) explanation is the emergence of a part(s) out of a formerly integrated whole and from this integrated whole, complimentary and unique part(s) emerge in relation to the other part(s) in the system. This definition of differentiation (Huisman) suggests an egalitarian approach to education with room for further evolution and growth.

Although external differentiation (Huisman et al., 1995) was created by the formation of the ITALs, Clark (1983) stated that differentiation occurred "horizontally and vertically, within institutions and among them" (p. 36). This internal and external approach, presented a system of tiered hierarchies (Clark). In Ontario, universities would be considered vertically differentiated from colleges because of how each institutional group approached the type of knowledge taught, that is, theory versus vocational (Skolnik, 2011). This perception placed colleges one tier below the universities (Skolnik). Further vertical and horizontal differentiation exists among the CAATs and ITALs because George Brown, Humber, and Seneca have ITAL designation, which allows them to offer more bachelor's degrees (Fallis, 2013). This leads to the next point in the discussion: defining and understanding institutional diversity in relation to differentiation.

Diversity. Birnbaum (1983) provided a foundational understanding of institutional diversity when he explained that his "book does not propose that there is a single or even a "best" definition of diversity-the concept itself is too diverse for that. But it does offer a new way of looking at the issue that is analytic and embedded into coherent conceptual framework" (p. xii). Birnbaum described internal diversity as differences within institutions whereas external diversity is the differences between institutions. Internal and external diversity were further defined and categorized into seven elements: programmatic, procedural, systemic, constituential, reputational, values and climate, and structural (Birnbaum). These seven diversity dimensions were broad and applicable within as well as among institutions (Birnbaum).

Huisman et al. (1995) took this notion one step further when he described diversity as a static process and differentiation as a dynamic one. For example, in applying Huisman's approach, when new colleges are added to the already existing body of colleges in Ontario, this is simply a static change, but when a college converts to an ITAL, then that is dynamic differentiation within the higher education system. The same can be said about new programs that are outside of the scope of the preestablished group of programs within the individual college. What makes the institutions and systems even more static or dynamic are the tangible and intangible elements that Teichler (2008) characterized as formal and informal diversity. Teichler (2006) explained that there were vertical and horizontal attributes of informal diversity, such as reputation and perceived quality of education, which were unquantifiable. Horizontal and vertical, formal and informal diversity encapsulate what defines an institution by tangible and intangible qualities. These tangible and intangible qualities are included in the presentation about the types of programs offered by the three colleges. The next section of this chapter presents Trow's (1973) theoretical framework and contextualizes differentiation and diversity as it pertains to *Ontario's Differentiation Policy Framework for Postsecondary Education* (OMTCU, 2013).

Theoretical Context. Trow's (1973) influential work explained that the demand for higher education grew because of a historical watershed moment—World War II—and changes during those moments in the character of populations that wanted access to postsecondary education after the war. As these populations grew and changed over time, so did the types of education they required (Trow, 1973). Higher education transitioned from elite to mass and then to universal access (Trow, 1973). The Second World War created the context for significant societal and educational changes in most parts of Canada as well (Dennison & Gallagher, 1986) with the creation of the CAATs historically positioned vertically below universities. In the early part of the 21st century, Trow (2005) remarked that all three types of higher education could and did coexist within the postsecondary system and "many institutions provide recognizable forms of all three side by side in the same institutions" (Trow, 2005, p. 6). Ontario colleges are mass-universal systems because they are more "comprehensive" with more "diverse standards" (Trow, 1973, p. 10) because of their original mandate to meet the needs of the local communities they inhabited and provide a large range of programs not offered at the university level (Ontario Department of Education, 1967). If the province of Ontario has achieved universal higher education (Fallis, 2013), then the next educational transition is the design of a differentiated system of higher education in the province, which may potentially negate the original purpose of the CAATs.

Trow (1973) explained that in advanced society, as the size and functions of higher education changed, so did the orientations within the academic profession. He described this growth, diversification, and expansion as a partial democratization of higher education. Within this democratization of education came the opposing viewpoints of which direction or position institutions should maintain or change (Trow, 1973). Academic orientations were presented as a typology, which defined the preferred position of the academics, and the institutions they represented (Trow, 1973). "Elitist reformers" (Trow, 1973, p. 30) is the term that applies to the direction in which Ontario's mass-universal college system has the potential to go in light of the framework. To better understand the term, Trow (1973) defined it as:

> A small but significant body of academic men [sic] who wish to preserve the unique role of Universities as elite centers for scholarship and research at its highest level, but who recognize the need for certain internal reform that

would reflect the changed map of learning and the changing relationships between higher education and the larger society. (pp. 30–31).

The term may be reworded as *elitist reformed institutions* whereby the CAATs are "elite centers" (Trow, 1973, p. 30) for vocational training and applied research, which is one of the "components of differentiation" (OMTCU, 2013, p.10) in the framework.

Differentiation and Diversity in the Framework

When the term differentiation appeared in the *Ontario's Differentiation Policy Framework for Postsecondary Education* document for the first time, a definition of the term was unavailable. Instead, it read, "The government's policy of differentiation sets the foundation for broader postsecondary *system transformation* [emphasis added] by publicly articulating government expectations and aligning the mandates of Ontario's Colleges and Universities with government priorities" (OMTCU, 2013, p.6). This statement explained why differentiation was required and how it would look in general wording. How can something be explained when it lacks a definition to build upon? It was implied that differentiation was external and vertical (Teichler, 2006; van Vught, 2008) in its approach. Next, the framework implied horizontal, internal differentiation when it stated, "our overriding goals for a differentiated system are to build on and help focus the well-established strengths of institutions, enable them to operate together as complementary parts of a whole" (OMTCU, 2013, p.6).

Colleges then were externally differentiated and internally diverse with a changed access mandate of affordable provincial access. Furthermore, one of the "components of differentiation" was articulated as follows: "Differentiation strengthens alignment between regional development needs and defined institutional mandates. This will advance innovative partnerships and programs that serve the distinct Ontario communities to which institutions are connected, as well as broader provincial needs" (p. 10). The functions of higher education were no longer for mass and local needs but for government needs (Trow, 1973).

These government needs were further outlined in the "program areas of institutional strength/specialization" (OMTCU, 2013, pp.10–11). The words "specialization" (p. 11) and "specialty" (p. 10) appeared once in each case. "Specialty" (p. 11) was used in the following context: "Institutions will focus on areas of educational strength and *specialty* [emphases added] that *collectively* they offer maximum choice, flexibility, and quality experience to Ontario students" (p. 10). The way the term was used suggested program diversity (Huisman et al., 1995). Also, the document (OMTCU, 2013) stated that higher education institutions needed to focus "on areas of program strength ... to define their role in the postsecondary education system ... that is responsive to student needs and regional demands, and

Table 2.1   Student Head Count by Institution and Credential (2013–2014)

| | Institution | | |
Credential	George Brown	Humber	Seneca
Certificate	2752	2655	2236
Degree (includes applied degree)	823	3313	1681
Diploma	11935	13798	12858
Total	15210	19922	16755

Source: Adapted from Ontario Ministry of Training, Colleges, and Universities (2014).

avoid unnecessary duplication" (p. 11). This unnecessary duplication affects the three colleges because as they become further differentiated, students will have limited options for entrance into a program(s) creating an environment of elitist exclusivity (Trow, 1973). This would jeopardize the democratization of education (Trow, 1973), unless the colleges are allowed to continue with their current comprehensive curriculum and create internally differentiated, elitist, specialized programs within these mass-universal, comprehensive colleges (Trow, 2005).

College Data

The framework outlined eight metrics for the differentiation that the colleges must respond to in the form of SMAs, in order to gauge the extent to which they were pursuing differentiation (which may affect their funding) (OMTCU, 2013). The eight metrics were a combination of institutional, as identified by the colleges, and systemwide metrics, as identified by the ministry (OMTCU, 2013). Furthermore, these institutional metrics were "rooted in historical data to enable measurement of progress over time" (OMTCU, 2013, p.13). Although the government metrics were "based on current data collected or already available to the ministry" (OMTCU, 2013, p.13), the combined components of measurement were jobs, innovation, and economic development; teaching and learning; student population; research and graduate education; program offerings, institutional collaboration to support student mobility; strategic enrolment and financial sustainability (OMTCU, 2013). The 2013–14 credentials awarded, program offerings, and student enrolment categories for George Brown, Humber, and Seneca suggested the type of differentiation and/or diversity these institutions exhibited.

Table 2.1 provides and compares the number of students in each college and category of credentials offered. It also highlights the most popular credential across the three colleges by student head count.

Tables 2.2 and 2.3 provide a gauge as to which programs garnered a high number of students. For the purposes of this chapter, only programs

Table 2.2   Student Head Count by Institution and Similar or Same Program (2013–2014)

	Institution		
Program	George Brown	Humber	Seneca
Architectural Technology	332	390	
Practical Nursing	438	452	459
Broadcasting—Radio, Film, Television, Journalism		507	109
Bachelor of Applied Arts (Film and Media Production)		210	
Business	498	2196	2204
Bachelor of Applied Business	419	348	600
Child and Youth Worker	374	438	302
Computer Technology	401		1178
Court, Tribunal, Administrative		461	263
Early Childhood		553	723
Engineering	691	433	763
Police Foundations		452	490
Total	3153	6440	7091

Source: Adapted from Ontario Ministry of Training, Colleges, and Universities (2014).

with 100 students or more were included. Table 2.3 illustrates some of the most popular programs grouped thematically together within each college and their total collective student head count.

The Road Ahead

Based on the data presented, these three colleges are mass-universal institutions with elitist-reformist characteristics manifesting in the form of differentiated programs and credentials within and among the colleges (Skolnik, 2013). The framework required that the colleges respond and provide a document that presented their various "institution-specific metrics" (OMTCU, 2013, p. 13). Under "Program Offerings" (p. 15), the subheading "Concentration of enrolment at Colleges by occupational cluster and by credential" (p. 15) is important when gauging the level of programmatic differentiation among and within these colleges. George Brown's SMA (2014) listed the following "Areas of Institutional Strength" (p. 8):

1. Culinary and Hospitality
2. Design
3. Construction
4. Community Health
5. Business Management
6. Business Marketing
7. Dental
8. Information and Communication

Table 2.3   Student Head Count by Institution and Differentiated Program (2013–2014)

		Institution			
Program	George Brown	Program	Humber	Program	Seneca
Apparel Manufacturing Management	253	Architectural Technology	390	Air Carrier/airport Management	103
Baking And Pastry Arts Management	144	Court and Tribunal Agent	461	Fire Protection Technician	103
Dental Assisting (levels I and Ii)	158	Fashion Arts— Modeling and Fashion	324	Fire Protection Technology	214
				Opticianry	160
Dental Hygiene	142	Funeral Service Education	101	Veterinary Technician	144
Dental Technology	122	Interior Decorating	148		
Fashion Business Industry	140				
Fashion Technique and Design	161				
Hearing Instrument Specialist	116				
Mechanical Engineering Technology— Tool and Machine	184				

Source: Adapted from Ontario Ministry of Training, Colleges, and Universities (2014).

9. Technology
10. Access and Immigrant Education

Humber's (2014, p. 8) included:

1. Media
2. Creative and Performing Arts
3. Design
4. Social Services
5. Law and Security
6. Health and Wellness
7. Nursing

NEW DIRECTIONS FOR COMMUNITY COLLEGES • DOI: 10.1002/cc

8. Business
9. Technology

And from Seneca (2014, p. 10):

1. Media, Fashion, and Design
2. Community Service
3. Information and Communications Technology
4. Business Management
5. Accounting and Finance
6. Marketing
7. Health and Wellness
8. Chemical/Biological Sciences
9. Engineering Technology
10. Aviation

These academic areas suggest the need for a clear and concise definition of differentiation because without one, an attempt to comply with the
framework will be problematic. On the one hand, formally differentiated institutions would be cost effective in terms of resources and expertise (Clark,
Trick, & Van Loon, 2011). On the other hand, differentiated institutions
offering specialized training can lead to a form of organizational fragmenta-
tion within the system and amongst similarly grouped institutions as they
move in that direction (Clark, 1983). Collaboration across institutions was
one of the key concepts emphasized in the framework but how could that
be accomplished if the colleges become specialized and no longer have
access to other programs or disciplines within the same institution? This
could potentially lead to steeper, unquantifiable, intangible institutional
differentiation (Teichler, 2006). Ontario's higher education system may
become figuratively and literally fractured and then what kind of mandate
would be required to mend it? Perhaps the solution to differentiation isn't
an institutional one but a programmatic one whereby these mass-universal
institutions house elite programs (Trow, 1973) yet still remain accessible to
all regardless of geographic location. Perhaps a responsive rather than reac-
tive differentiated higher education framework would be beneficial for all.

References

Birnbaum, R. (1983). *Maintaining diversity in higher education*. San Francisco, CA:
Jossey-Bass.
Clark, B. R. (1983). *The higher education system: Academic organization in cross-national
perspective*. Berkeley, CA: University of California Press.
Clark, I. D., Moran, G., Skolnik, M. L., & Trick, D. (2009). *Academic transformation:
The forces reshaping higher education in Ontario*. Montreal, Quebec; Kingston, Ontario:
McGill-Queen's University Press.

Clark, I. D., Trick, D., & Van Loon, R. (2011). *Academic reform: Policy options for improving the quality and cost-effectiveness of undergraduate education in Ontario.* Montreal, Quebec: School of Policy Studies, Queen's University.

Dennison, J. D., & Gallagher, P. (1986). *Canada's community colleges: A critical analysis.* Vancouver, British Columbia: University of British Columbia Press.

Fallis, G. (2013). *Rethinking higher education: Participation, research and differentiation.* Montreal, Quebec; Kingston, Ontario: McGill-Queen's University Press.

George Brown College. (2014). *Strategic mandate agreement (2014–17).* Retrieved from http://www.tcu.gov.on.ca/pepg/publications/vision/GeorgeBrownSMA.pdf

Huisman, J., & Centrum voor Studies van het Hoger Onderwijsbeleid (Enschede, Netherlands). (1995). *Differentiation, diversity, and dependency in higher education: A theoretical and empirical analysis.* Utrecht, The Netherlands: Uitgeverij Lemma BV.

Humber College. (2014). *Strategic mandate agreement (2014–17).* Retrieved from http://www.tcu.gov.on.ca/pepg/publications/vision/HumberSMA.pdf

Kymlicka, B. B. (1978). Ontario. In E. Sheffield, D. D. Campbell, J. Holmes, B. B. Kymlicka, & J. H. Whitelaw (Eds.), *Systems of higher education: Canada* (pp. 101–132). New York: Interbook Inc.

Ontario Department of Education. (1967). *Basic documents.* Ottawa, Ontario: Ontario Department of Education.

Ontario Ministry of Training, Colleges, and Universities. (2013). *Ontario's differentiation policy framework for postsecondary education.* Retrieved fromhttp://www.tcu.gov.on.ca/pepg/publications/PolicyFramework_PostSec.pdf

Ontario Ministry of Training, Colleges, and Universities. (2014). Enrolment statistical reporting. Retrieved from http://www.ontario.ca/data/college-enrolment

Seneca College. (2014). *Strategic mandate agreement (2014–17).* Retrieved fromhttp://www.tcu.gov.on.ca/pepg/publications/vision/SenecaSMA.pdf

Skolnik, M. L. (2011). Re-conceptualizing the relationship between community colleges and universities using a conceptual framework drawn from the study of jurisdictional conflict between professions. *Community College Review, 39*(4), 352–375.

Skolnik, M. L. (2013). An historical perspective on the idea of institutional diversity and differentiation in Ontario higher education. *College Quarterly, 16*(2). Retrieved from http://collegequarterly.ca/2013-vol16-num02-spring/skolnik.html

Teichler, U. (2006). Changing structures of the higher education systems: The increasing complexity of underlying forces. *Higher Education Policy, 19*(4), 447–461.

Teichler, U. (2008). Diversification? Trends and explanations of the shape and size of higher education. *Higher Education, 56*(3), 349–379.

Trow, M. (1973). *Problems in the transition from elite to mass higher education.* Berkeley, CA: Carnegie Commission on Higher Education.

Trow, M. (2005). *Reflections on the transition from elite to mass to universal access: Forms and phases of higher education in modern societies since WWII* (Institute of Governmental Studies Working Papers). Berkeley, CA: University of California.

van Vught, F. (2008). Mission diversity and reputation in higher education. *Higher Education Policy, 21,* 151–174.

HELEN SIANOS *is an interdisciplinary professor at Centennial College in Toronto, Ontario, Canada. She is currently a PhD student in the Department of Leadership, Adult and Higher Education at the Ontario Institute for Studies in Education, University of Toronto.*

NEW DIRECTIONS FOR COMMUNITY COLLEGES • DOI: 10.1002/cc

3

This chapter describes the results of case study research on a partnership between a community college in the United States and a university in Chile that attempted to develop the first community college system in Chile.

A Partnership for a Community College in Chile

Carmen L. McCrink, Heidi Whitford

The American community college stands as a symbol of democracy based on its open-door mission and thus, the granting of access to a diverse population including the nontraditional as well as traditional student. Currently, the nontraditional student may be returning to school after several years, represent one of many ethnic and racial identities, be classified as an undocumented immigrant, and depend on financial assistance in order to pursue postsecondary education. Indeed, the historiography of higher education in the United States across the last 300 years attests to the transformation from what was originally an elite system of education for the privileged classes during the colonial era, to one which attempts to promote the essence of social justice. A comprehensive review of the 1947 President's Commission on Higher Education highlights the framing of policy agendas, which aimed at underscoring access and equity through specific initiatives, such as the ending of racial and religious discrimination; eliminating financial barriers; and expanding the role of community colleges through the development and implementation of the transfer function (Gilbert & Heller, 2013). Hence, the term, "junior college," originally used to identify this type of institution, was replaced by "community college" (Gilbert & Heller).

In this second decade of the 21st century, community colleges in the United States enroll approximately one third of degree-seeking students (Weiss et al., 2014). The question often raised is why attend a community college? To begin with, these institutions position the student at the center by framing agendas for persistence through a myriad of services for a successful academic experience. Recent initiatives that have been launched to foster community college students' degree attainment include partnerships within states, such as the Path to Accelerated Completion and

NEW DIRECTIONS FOR COMMUNITY COLLEGES, no. 177, Spring 2017 © 2017 Wiley Periodicals, Inc.
Published online in Wiley Online Library (wileyonlinelibrary.com) • DOI: 10.1002/cc.20239

Employment and the Arkansas Trade Adjustment Assistance Community College and Career Training Grant, which has as one its goals to "reduce time to completion and unnecessary credit accumulation and to improve job placement" (Smith, Baldwin, & Schmidt, 2015, p. 33). Additional ventures include the development, implementation, and sustainability of articulation agreements between community colleges and universities that enable students to transfer vertically. The acceptance of community college credits in a program of study by the senior institution (university) that confers the baccalaureate degree underscores the context of a seamless transition (O'Meara, Hall, & Carmichael, 2007).

Internationalization, in response to globalization forces, now affects all sectors of the socioeconomic and political infrastructure, including higher education institutions. This new landscape provides a fertile terrain for the extension of educational ventures beyond national borders and thus the development of partnerships and articulation agreements between countries and postsecondary institutions. Clearly, the initiation of global agreements between institutions has served to "facilitate the sharing of knowledge, the transfer of technologies, and the mobility of students, academics, researchers, and administrators focusing on training, employment, and scientific knowledge" (Figueroa, 2008, p. 64).

Within this context, the purpose of this research was to study the newly developed community college system in Chile. For the purposes of this study, pseudonyms have been used for the institutions involved in the case study, which were as follows: National University (NU) in Chile, the American Community College (ACC) in the United States, and the resulting entity formed by the partnership: the Community College of Chile (CCC). The lens of organizational learning theory was used as a guiding framework. The overarching question guiding this qualitative research was as follows: What are the perceptions of administrators and faculty members involved in the formation of the partnership regarding the formation of the new community college in Chile? Subquestions were as follows: What governance structures are in place at ACC to promote the traditional mission of the American community college system? How do programs of study at ACC align with workforce entry requirements in Chile? What is the relationship between stakeholders at ACC and NU? The resulting interviews with faculty and administrators who participated in the partnership illustrated the multifaceted, complex relationships and processes that led toward the development of the CCC.

Literature Review

This literature review provides an overview of the higher education system in Chile, vis-à-vis the recent student movements in Chile; addresses issues pertaining to the development of cross-border partnerships between postsecondary institutions; and explores the role of organizational learning as the theoretical framework for the study.

Higher Education in Chile Today: The Neoliberal Ethos. In 1981, the postsecondary education system in Chile experienced a major restructuring that culminated in the establishment of four types of institutions: "universities, professional institutes, technical training centers, and institutions of higher education for the armed forces" (Espinoza & González, 2008, p. 201). In an effort to fully understand the current crisis in higher education in Chile and the ensuing student movements, it is imperative to place the 1981 reform within the context of the Pinochet dictatorship (1973–1990), following the aftermath of the Allende overthrow (Goldberg, 1975). Whereas Allende's policy agendas favored the poor and working-class citizens, across all sectors including higher education, the Pinochet regime sought to develop and implement a neoliberal economic structure focused on privatization and a free-market paradigm (Cabalin, 2012).

The two Chilean student movements, the "Penguin Revolution" in 2006 and the "Chilean Winter" in 2011, were in direct response to this mantra of privatization and inequality. Prior to the onset the 2011 student movement, a partnership between American Community College in the United States and National University in Chile was established to create one of the first community college systems in South America—the Community College of Chile—under the auspices of the National University. This dialogue between the two institutions and subsequent partnership appeared to recognize the need to advocate for equality and access to higher education, on the part of Chilean administrators and faculty, through emulating the American community college system by offering 2-year degrees in specific technical careers, while providing exposure to a university environment and the possibility of transfer to a baccalaureate program.

Cross-Border Partnerships. Postsecondary institutions around the globe are now part of an ecological system that demands revolutionary change and adaptation of new modalities for survival in a highly competitive international environment (Kirst & Stevens, 2015). The success of these partnerships is based upon a commitment to collaboration between institutions and the identification of common goals by stakeholders on both sides (Duffield, Olson, & Kerzman, 2012). Several elements must be present toward sustaining the partnership including the following: the openness among constituencies (Duffield, Olson, & Kerzman), faculty involvement and collaboration in curriculum development (Chiteng Kot, 2014), and awareness of differences in learning behaviors of administrators and faculty involved in the project (Waterval, Frambach, Driessen, & Scherpbier, 2015). In essence, successful partnerships stem from those institutional contexts that promote organizational learning and create collaborative teams to create a beneficial experience for students that takes into account the cultures and languages of the two institutions (Waterval et al., 2015).

NEW DIRECTIONS FOR COMMUNITY COLLEGES • DOI: 10.1002/cc

Organizational Learning. The seminal work of Argyris and Schön (1978) is focused on a "theory of action," which suggests that organizations must be ready to engage in change, whether this be evolutionary or revolutionary in nature, and, it is hoped, learn through these change processes. Within this context, there are two types of learning, which Argyris and Schön refer to as either single loop or double loop. Whereas single-loop learning aims at detecting errors within the organization, yet maintaining "control over immediate task, rules, and structures" (Fiol & Lyles, 1985, p. 810), double-loop learning sometimes demands the possible restructuring of organizational norms and/or strategies (Argyris & Schön, 1978). In essence, double-loop learning requires systemic change. Bauman (2005) adapted Argyris and Schön's theory to postsecondary institutions and underscored three factors as prerequisites for organizational learning: "the presence of new ideas, the cultivation of doubt in existing knowledge and practices, and the development and transfer of knowledge among institutional actors" (p. 25).

When reflecting on organizational learning theory, it becomes clear that for higher levels of learning (double loop) to take place in postsecondary institutions, especially those that have entered into partnerships across borders, a sense of collaboration and receptiveness to innovation or discovery, as well as a willingness to adopt a different institutional direction, must be present for long-lasting success and the ultimate transformation of institutional agendas.

Methodology

The research strategy used for this project was a case study design (Yin, 2009). Case study methodology was selected because it facilitates an in-depth understanding of a problem or question situated within a case through multiple forms of data collection and analysis. Case study research uses a variety of data to inform the primary research questions in order to explore the form that organizational learning takes within the formation of a community college in Chile following the U.S. model. For this study, data were collected from the institutions involved in the formation of the Community College of Chile, including National University in Chile, and the American Community College in the United States. Documents comprised part of the data, as well as interviews with various stakeholders from the institutions that comprised the case.

The case study focused on the analysis of interview data, as well as pertinent documents such as minutes of meetings, proposed curricula, reports, and related archival data. The researchers conducted open-ended interviews (via Skype) with key participants from among American Community College administrators and faculty who were involved in the development of the Community College of Chile partnership. The data were uploaded into Nvivo software for analysis, which consisted of coding the data for common themes. The documents collected were analyzed using a content analysis method informed by Krippendorff (2012), which provided prescriptions for analyzing document-derived data that focus on exploring patterns and relationships among the data from different sources. Guided by principles of thematic and narrative analysis (Merriam, 1998; Riessman, 2008), the context of the case was described in terms of relationships, connections, and patterns that emerged between the entities within the case. These elements were described, cataloged, and analyzed to form a complete picture of the case and the subunits within it.

Findings and Analysis

The research findings and analyses are presented in response to the overarching and subquestions. The overarching research question inquired about the perceptions of administrators and faculty members at ACC and NU regarding a partnership to form a community college in Chile. A number of themes emerged that describe the findings related to the overarching research question as well as the subquestions that were derived from interviews with ACC administrators and faculty. These themes included the need for open dialogue and a free exchange of ideas between the partnership members, as well as a collaborative response to unforeseen challenges. In addition, the collaborative partnership included being receptive to a culture of learning, as well as promoting the ideal of an inclusive form of higher education following the "open access" model of the U.S. community college model. Finally, the analysis led to themes including degree programs and articulation agreements, as well as the relationship of collaboration among the stakeholders in the partnership.

Open Dialogue and Exchange of Ideas.   The participants in the partnership described open dialogue and exchange of ideas as the driving force for the partnership. Participants indicated that both institutions initially agreed on the benefits of a partnership structure and the desire for a dual-degree program that focused on curriculum alignment. One participant stated:

> We would exchange ideas and students... The NU would send their English speaking students who wanted to become teachers to learn English. The students' experience at ACC was very different from their experience in Chile... They were our best ambassadors. We developed a relationship with NU's administration. (Participant 1)

This response is indicative of a desire for openness during the preliminary stages of the partnership as part of the criteria for success as discussed by Duffield et al. (2012).

Another participant discussed the personal connections that led to the development of the partnership: "We began because of a personal

connection with one of the faculty members here, and one of his students."
(Participant 3). This participant described how faculty and students from
both countries formed connections between ACC in the United States and
the partnership institution, NU, in Chile.

Emergence of Unpredictable Challenges.   Participants listed a number of unanticipated challenges that surfaced after the official opening of
the Community College of Chile in 2010. These included the following:
(a) lack of familiarity with the transfer function based on the history of education in Chile—specifically, the positioning of technical careers as "terminal" and not associated with a university degree; (b) faculty members'
perception of teaching and unfamiliarity with student-centered models; (c)
student movements—namely, the 2011 "Chilean Winter"; and (d) continuous turmoil in NU's administration as the board of trustees took control
over the administration and faculty based on political ideologies. Participants' comments with reference to these challenges were as follows:

> The disconnect between Chile not having a community college system (they
> have a technical school system) and the concept of transferring credits did
> not exist. (Participant 1)

> They were just totally different in the manner of teaching. In Chile, it's very
> hierarchical teaching. (Participant 1)

> The higher education system in Chile is traditional. You want to become a
> lawyer, or a doctor, you are on a track. If you want to change professions, you
> have to start all over again . . . credits do not transfer. (Participant 2)

> There is no financial aid system speak of . . . Students started protesting that
> they wanted a free education. (Participant 1)

> When the students started taking the university buildings and protesting
> against the administration, the president of the university was not really vo-
> cal against the students. and that was considered by the board of trustees as
> a president that was not acting according to the wishes of the board. (Partic-
> ipant 2)

These narratives speak to the need for collaboration, at the onset of
a partnership, toward informing agendas for the development of organizational learning across both institutions (Kezar, 2005; Waterval et al., 2015).

Culture of Learning.   Inquiries into the structure of governance or
the organizational culture at ACC resulted in findings that related the traditional mission of the American community college system to the formation
of the community college in Chile. Participants described the organizational
culture at ACC as "inclusive," "collegial," and "transparent."

NEW DIRECTIONS FOR COMMUNITY COLLEGES • DOI: 10.1002/cc

American Community College has always been rated as one of the most innovative community colleges. (Participant 1)

American Community College is a great place. The faculty are very committed
to innovation. I always feel proud of being a faculty member at this college.
From the moment this college was created, I would say that from the administration down to the last faculty member that was hired were involved in
learning. (Participant 2)

ACC has a commitment to social justice both in the US and elsewhere. It
aligns with our sense that ACC is a very international place because of the
student body and the way in which we should be supportive of community
colleges elsewhere was very much in line with our mission. (Participant 3)

A big chunk of the conversation was to sell them the ACC model. To explain
to them that it was not a technical school, that it was more than a technical
school. (Participant 5).

As these statements show, ACC has a very strong organizational culture
that aligns with the overarching mission of the community college system of
the United States: One that is open access, supportive of social justice, and
committed to innovative ideas. In addition, the aforementioned statements
also describe the active role of faculty participation in collaboration with
the partnership to create a community college in Chile.

Access to Higher Education.   Providing access to higher education
for low-income and nontraditional students is a fundamental mission of the
American community college model. An upper-level administrator at ACC
who was interviewed expounded on how ACC focused on the educational
needs of low-income and nontraditional students and how this mission also
transferred to the development of the partnership in Chile. She stated:

Women in Chile, in particular low-income women, have very little access
to higher education; there is an enormous well of support for activities that
would address these issues. (Participant 3)

In Chile they have a very elite system of higher education, where the elite
send their children, and they are very traditionally aged and have a European
style of education. The community college flies in the face of that in a couple
of ways. It is not elite. To expand the ecosystem you've really got to get in
there create these new systems. (Participant 3)

These quotes demonstrate the commitment of ACC to open access
higher education, and also the need for it in Chile.

Degree Programs and Articulation Agreements.   An exploration
of programs of study at ACC and NU revealed the relationship between

academic programs of study and workforce entry requirements in Chile. For example, dual-degree programs in Chile focused on "technical" careers in business, mining, and teaching. NU wanted to recruit students to be part of the new community college in Chile and send them to ACC to receive part of their education and bolster their skill levels, as illustrated in the following quotes:

> NU wanted to recruit students for good jobs, mining jobs, and send them to ACC. The NU had an engineering school and for them this was a group project. Some of the students have very high GPAs when they arrived at ACC. (Participant 1)

> And the mining sector was so enthusiastic they were willing to give money to set up, almost like a lab, inside the Community College of Chile. (Participant 1)

> One of the conditions that was always present was that the dean at NU wanted a dual program. For him this was extremely important. (Participant 2)

> When they (NU) sent their faculty to ACC, my job was to show them how to get [funding] for technology. How you go to private industry based on their need for certain skilled laborers and then get them to pay for the equipment. (Participant 1).

ACC and NU operated under an articulation agreement in which credits taken at the new community college of Chile could be examined by the Transfer Evaluation Office at ACC, so that if Chilean students wished to transfer to ACC at some point in the future, they would be able to do so and get credit for the courses they took at the Community College of Chile.

A participant who was part of the Transfer Evaluation Office at ACC remarked that part of the collaborative effort to form a working partnership agreement with the CCC involved the creation of an articulation agreement. However, this collaboration went far beyond just an articulation agreement. For example, ACC intended to assist visiting Chilean students with room, board, and transportation in order to facilitate the visiting students with finishing their degrees at ACC. Participant 4 stated: "To have a partnership, you have to have all parties involved in the process, in terms of articulation between programs." In addition, many ACC students took classes at NU or at the Community College of Chile as exchange students and received credits toward their degree program at ACC. However, not all credits taken in Chile were recognized by ACC. For instance, English classes taken in Chile were not recognized for credit at ACC.

Stakeholder Relationships.   An important part of the investigation of this partnership involved exploring the relationships between stakeholders. Differences between the two educational systems in the United States and

Chile led to resistance and lack of sustainability for the newly formed community college in Chile. Participants shared that, albeit initially the NU administration and faculty were receptive and welcoming of best practices of ACC, historical differences in teaching methodology as well as lack of understanding and familiarity with the role of a community college served to maintain the status quo, in which nonuniversity postsecondary education was fulfilled by technical institutes in Chile. Eventually, the newly formed Community College of Chile ceased to exist and was replaced by a technical institute.

> So business people [in Chile] understand the need for community colleges whereas the traditional faculty at UC think of the community college as the enemy of higher education. (Participant 1)

> There was a fear among the faculty that a community college, that these students moving up [transferring to a baccalaureate program] would be inferior educationally. There was a fear that the level of education would go down and they wanted to use the term "technical." (Participant 1)

> Today the community college doesn't exist; they changed the name to "Instituto de Carreras Tecnicas." (Participant 2)

> Is it a bad model or a good model? If it didn't work, does that help people? I think we now understand how we would do things differently. I really do like the idea of working side by side with people who are interested in colleges in developing countries and saying, "we know as Americans how it works for us, but we don't know your context." (Participant 3)

These narratives address the need to identify the cultural and sociological factors that might be germane to each country, including familiarity with its history and political ideologies, at the very onset of developing relationships, as these might have an impact on the outcome or sustainability of the project (Duffield et al., 2012; Waterval et al., 2015).

Conclusions and Recommendations for Practice

The findings of this study serve to illuminate those factors that must be taken into account when developing cross-border partnerships within the context of postsecondary institutions. First, an open dialogue between institutions needs to include an awareness of each country's historiography from a socioeconomic perspective, vis-à-vis political ideologies, and how these may have a direct impact as to who should have access to higher education. Clearly, in certain countries, social status will determine an individual's path toward direct entry into the workforce or the university. Educators across the United States must unequivocally understand that the

New Directions for Community Colleges • DOI: 10.1002/cc

community college system—with the open door and a transfer function—
is germane to a democratic ideology and, as such, it may not always be
transferable to other countries. Second, stakeholders need to establish
relationships with specific entities and/or affiliations across countries in an
effort to have these serve in the role of ambassadors toward new initiatives.
Participants shared that this was part of the learning process.

> One thing that was important and we learned [for future ventures] is getting
> the U.S. Embassy and the U.S. Department of Commerce involved. (Partici-
> pant 1)

> If you're interested in talking to Catholic universities in Chile, there are sev-
> eral of them. You can explore with them the idea of a community college.
> (Participant 2)

Third, stakeholders must become aware of the governance models that
might be evident at each institution and how these may, or may not, be
instrumental toward developing a culture of learning. Indeed, double-loop
learning or change in institutional mission requires a willingness for innovation and a drift away from bureaucratic strategies. Fourth, faculty members who wish to participate in the partnership must exchange ideas and
collaborate on curriculum matters as well as teaching methodology toward building consensus for the implementation of an institutional or systemwide change on the part of either partner.

As could be seen from the statements made by the participants from the
ACC side of the partnership, mistakes were made, but overall, it was a positive learning experience that led them to be open to further international
partnerships in the future. Findings from this study may serve to inform
community college administrators and faculty of specific strategies toward
the development of partnerships abroad, while emphasizing the merits of
a community college system to meet the country's industry demands and
access to postsecondary education.

References

Argyris, C., & Schön, D. A. (1978). *Organizational learning: A theory of action perspective.*
    Reading, MA: Addison-Wesley Publishing Company.
Bauman, G. L. (2005). Promoting organizational learning in higher education to achieve
    equity in educational outcomes. In A. Kezar (Ed.), *New Directions for Higher Educa-
    tion: No. 131. Organizational learning in higher education* (pp. 23–35). San Francisco,
    CA: Jossey-Bass.
Cabalin, C. (2012). Neoliberal education and student movements in Chile: Inequalities
    and malaise. *Policy Futures in Education, 10*(2), 219–228.
Chiteng Kot, F. (2014). Stakeholder participation in international higher education part-
    nerships: results of a survey of two sub-Saharan African universities. *Tertiary Educa-
    tion and Management, 20*(3), 252–272.

Duffield, S., Olson, A., & Kerzman, R. (2012). Crossing borders, breaking boundaries: Collaboration among higher education institutions. *Innovative Higher Education, 38,* 237–250. doi:10.1007/s10755-012-9238-8

Espinoza, O., & Gonzalez, L. E. (2013). Access to higher education in Chile: Public vs. private analysis. *Prospects, 43,* 199–214. doi:10.1007/s11125-013-9268-8

Fiol, C. M., & Lyles, M. A. (1985). Organizational learning. *The Academy of Management Review, 10*(4), 803–813.

Figueroa, F. E. (2008). European influences in Chilean and Mexican higher education: The Bologna Process and the Tuning Project, *European Education, 40*(1), 63–77.

Gilbert, C. K., & Heller, D. E. (2013). Access, equity, and community colleges: The Truman commission and federal higher education policy from 1947 to 2011. *Journal of Higher Education, 84*(3), 417–443.

Goldberg, P. A. (1975). The politics of the Allende overthrow in Chile. *Political Science Quarterly, 90*(1), 93–116.

Kezar, A. (Ed.). (2005). Organizational learning in higher education. *New Directions for Higher Education, 131.*

Kirst, M. W., & Stevens, M. L. (2015). *Remaking college: The changing ecology of higher education.* Stanford, CA: Stanford University Press.

Krippendorff, K. (2012). *Content analysis: An introduction to its methodology.* Thousand Oaks, CA: Sage.

Merriam, S. B. (1998). *Qualitative research and case study applications in education.* San Francisco, CA: Jossey-Bass.

O'Meara, R., Hall, T., & Carmichael, M. (2007). A discussion of past, present, and future articulation models at postsecondary institutions. *Journal of Technology Studies, 33*(1), 9–16.

Riessman, C. K. (2008). *Narrative methods for the human sciences.* Thousand Oaks, CA: Sage.

Smith, C. A., Baldwin, C., & Schmidt, G. (2015, March–April). Student success centers: Leading the charge for change at community colleges. *Change,* 30–39.

Waterval, D. G. J., Frambach, J. M., Driessen, E. W., & Scherpbier, A. J. J. A. (2015). Copy but not paste: A literature review of crossborder curriculum partnerships. *Journal of Studies in International Education, 19*(1), 65–85. doi:10.1177/10283153114533608

Weiss, M. J., Mayer, A., Cullinan, D., Ratledge, A, Sommo, C., & Diamond, J. (2014). *A random assignment evaluation of learning communities seven years later: Impacts on education and earnings outcomes.* Paper presented at the Society for Research on Educational Effectiveness, Evanston, IL. Abstract retrieved from http://eric.ed.gov/?q=ED562717

Yin, R. K. (2009). *Case study research: Design and methods* (Vol. 5). Thousand Oaks, CA: Sage.

CARMEN L. MCCRINK *is associate professor and chair of the Higher Education Administration Department at Barry University, Miami Shores, Florida.*

HEIDI WHITFORD *is an assistant professor in the Higher Education Administration Department at Barry University, Miami Shores, Florida.*

This chapter provides an overview of community colleges in mainland China, addressing briefly the recent history of community college development, defining these institutions, detailing various models with examples, and discussing challenges faced by these institutions and recommendations for future development.

Models of Community Colleges in Mainland China

Yi (Leaf) Zhang

Although the American community college model is historically a unique concept to North America, it has been gradually adopted in other nations and regions (Cohen, Brawer, & Kisker, 2014). In fact, community-college-like institutions around the world have grown exponentially and have made key contributions to higher education expansion and economic development (Fleishman & Luo, 2013). Mainland China (hereafter China) is no exception to adopt this new trend, especially when it is facing rapidly growing demands for a well-educated workforce. As Premier Li Keqiang addressed to vocational educators in 2014, the skilled workforce is indispensable to boost "made in China" to "high-quality manufacturing" (Central People's Government, 2014, para 1).

China drew upon the achievements of the U.S. community colleges to advance its postsecondary vocational education and to promote lifelong learning. China has undertaken great efforts in developing its own community college system (Liu, 2013). However, understanding China's community colleges can be challenging, because these institutions were developed in different educational sectors, emerged following dissimilar patterns, and carry a variety of names.

To better depict the community college movement in China, this chapter first focuses on the development of community colleges, providing a brief introduction to the background of the evolvement of community colleges in China. It then discusses definition of these institutions. Next, the chapter highlights diversity of the community colleges with examples of various models. Finally, this chapter concludes with challenges and

New Directions for Community Colleges, no. 177, Spring 2017 © 2017 Wiley Periodicals, Inc.
Published online in Wiley Online Library (wileyonlinelibrary.com) • DOI: 10.1002/cc.20240

suggestions for further development of China's community college system and future research focusing on this line of inquiry.

Development of China's Community Colleges

China's interests in developing community colleges can be traced back to the early 1980s, when the nation opened itself to the outside world seeking approaches to realize national modernization (Postiglione, 2009). To achieve such an ambitious goal, demands on an educated labor market have been rapidly increasing. Traditional higher education institutions have been facing challenges to respond to such demands. Consequently, reform in higher education was urged to produce more skilled and knowledgeable workers (McBreen, McBreen, & Wu, 1996).

China turned itself to educational systems in other countries for innovative ideas to reform its higher education. China examined a variety of systems of vocational education, including German technical and dual-system vocational colleges, Australia's technical and further education, and other vocational institutions in France, South Korea, and Japan (Fleishman & Luo, 2013; Postiglione, 2009). China gave special attention to the U.S. community college model and recognized its prominent characteristics, such as building connections between the college and the community, offering flexible schedules and programs, and providing a wide variety of educational opportunities and credentials (Postiglione, 2009). It is believed that integrating these characteristics into China's higher education can better accommodate diverse interests from all walks of life, better satisfy the training and educational needs of the local community, and ultimately better respond to the increased demands of a skilled workforce in China. Consequently, the U.S. concept, along with the others, has been adopted by China's higher education to advance and expand its existing vocational and technical colleges.

Additionally, the central government and educational authorities have explored new models to develop community colleges that can not only foster vocational education but also promote lifelong learning. A considerable number of institutions that include "community college" in their titles have been established upon or transformed from postsecondary or secondary institutions. There is a dramatic increase in numbers of these institutions in the past 2 decades. Since the first community college was founded in 1994, 421 community colleges had been established by January 2013 (Liu, 2013).

Defining Community Colleges

Researchers, educators, and leaders of higher education attempt to define what a community college is in the Chinese context. For example, Liu (2013) defines a community college as a comprehensive higher education institution, focusing on specialized education and offering formal academic, vocational, continuing, and social and cultural education. The president of Beijing Chaoyang District Community College (Sun, 2005) believes that a community college is a local higher education institution that is led by the district government, responsive to the needs of local economic and social development, serves primarily youth and adults in the district, and offers collegial, adult, vocational, and community education in credit or noncredit programs.

Instead of proposing a definition, Postiglione (2009) describes China's community colleges with the following characteristics: (a) they are responsive to a specific geographical community; (b) the curriculum is more determined by the local needs; (c) they are more vocational-technical oriented; (d) they offer both part-time and full-time programs but highlight the former; (e) they are open to both adult learners and school leavers; and (f) they offer preparatory programs for self-study examination. Postiglione also indicates that, although most of the community colleges are public, the number of private ones is rapidly increasing and some collaborate with the public institutions.

Although these descriptions offer different perspectives, they all concur on main features of China's community colleges. Nevertheless, one can be easily confused when attempting to determine whether an institution is a community college, because the name of an institution does not necessarily reflect its characteristics (Postiglione, 2009). This creates additional difficulties when examining types of community colleges in China. The following section highlights important models that are often found in China's community colleges.

Exploring Community College Models in China

The concept of community college is not totally new to China. Many types of institutions in the vocational education sector resemble U.S. community colleges, such as 2- or 3-year vocational colleges, polytechnic colleges, regional or district colleges, and technical colleges (Raby, 1996, 2009). Particularly, China's higher professional and technical colleges (HPTCs, *gaodeng zhiye jishu xueyuan*) are generally referred to as counterparts of U.S. community colleges (Postiglione, 2009).

HPTCs focus on various technical specialized programs as well as general education. Most of these institutions are publically funded, but an increasing number of them seek private and social resources to function effectively (Postiglione, 2009). These institutions provide students with 2- or 3-year diplomas (*dazhuan*) upon their successful fulfillment of the college requirements. Although these diplomas are different from U.S. associate degrees, they play a similar role in job placement. Students with these diplomas become more competitive in the job market than those without any credentials (Roggow, 2014). A distinction between HPTCs and U.S. community colleges is access to 4-year universities (Yang, 2004). Unlike

NEW DIRECTIONS FOR COMMUNITY COLLEGES • DOI: 10.1002/cc

the open-door policy adopted by U.S. community colleges, HPTCs allow only a small group of students, who successfully pass certain screening procedures, to continue studying in a baccalaureate degree program *within* their city or province (Fleishman & Luo, 2013; Kong & Gimmestad, 1999).

In additional to HPTCs, there are over 400 named "community colleges" across mainland China and the number has been continuously growing. Most of these institutions emerged from adult education institutions under state or local governments, which hold the largest proportion of part-time students (Postiglione, 2009). Adult higher education consists of a wide variety of institutions, such as radio and television universities (RTVUs), cadre management colleges specializing in different industry and services (e.g., Guangxi Cadres University of Economics and Management, China Civil Aviation Management Institute, Hunan Economic Management Cadre College, etc.), Communist Party cadre colleges, and workers' colleges (Postiglione, Wang, & Watkins, 2015). Compared with HPTCs, community colleges are less investigated and thus their function and types remain unclear. The following section introduces some common models that have been developed under the label of "community college" in China.

Workers' Colleges and Universities (*zhigong xueyuan or daxue*). Numerous community colleges were built upon workers' colleges and universities, which have played an important role in training and educating skilled workers in certain industries. These institutions were first founded in the early 1980s and are governed directly by state-owned enterprises. Students graduating from workers' colleges can receive certificates, diplomas, or bachelor's degrees (Ju, 2007). Jinshan Community College in Shanghai is an example. It was formerly known as the Sinopec Shanghai Petrochemical Company Employees' College, which was built in the early 1970s. To explore the best ways to advance economic development, Shanghai municipal government decided to set up few community colleges as model institutions (Tao, 2001). Established in 1994, Jinshan was the first experiment; it is actually the first institution named as a "community college" in the entire mainland China. Jinshan Community College provides a wide variety of programs generally serving local citizens, including older adults, unemployed workers, and K–12 students. Since the inception of Jinshan Community College, Shanghai gradually developed a citywide community college system. By 2008, each of the 19 districts/counties in Shanghai had established its own community college.

Radio and Television Universities (RTVUs, *guangbo dianshi daxue*). As open and distance education institutions, RTVUs rank first in size in mega-universities in the world (Yang, 2011). RTVUs are operated at four levels: central (ministry of education), provincial, city, and district/county/industry. Most of these institutions have physical buildings, centers, or campuses where students attend classes or consult tutors. The name of RTVUs reflects the institutions' heritage. Founded in late 1970s, RTVUs delivered distance education predominantly through radio and television during their early years. With the development of technology, RTVUs today offer courses through a wide variety of media, including radio, television, print, audiovisual materials, and computer networks (Zhang & Shin, 2002). To reflect the new development in distance education, the China Central RTVU has changed its name to the Open University of China in 2012 (CCRTVU, n.d.). RTVUs offer both credit and noncredit programs. Students graduating from the credit programs receive 2- or 3-year college diplomas, which are considered by the government as equivalent to the type of diplomas conferred by regular colleges (Wei, 1997).

An increasing number of community colleges have been established on RTVUs' campuses (Liu, 2008). For instance, Zhejiang (Province) RTVU, which consists of 1 central campus, 9 directly governed branch campuses, 10 city RTVUs, and 59 county RTVUs, is one of the RTVU systems that has explored innovative ways to incorporate a community education component in their mission. From early 2008, Zhejiang RTVU started building community colleges at each level of its campuses and it has developed 11 city community colleges and 54 county community colleges by now (Zhejiang RTVU, n.d.). Most of these community colleges coexist with the local RTVUs. According to the institutional websites, RTVUs focus primarily on degree-bearing programs, whereas the community colleges highlight noncredit, lifelong learning opportunities for the local residents.

Adult Secondary Schools. In addition to postsecondary institutions, some community colleges were developed from adult secondary schools. These schools, which were originally focused on teaching intermediate workforce skills, have been upgraded to multipurpose colleges that aim to satisfy more local demands in economic and social development.

In the city of Wuhan, Wuchang Community Education College (WCEC, *Wuchangqu shequ jiaoyu xueyuan*) was developed from Wuchang District Adult Specialized Vocational Junior School (Liu, 2013). This vocational school was first established in 1984, preparing specialized talents for the local district. To respond to the central government's calls to create a learning society and to promote lifelong education, Wuchang Community Education College was formally created in 2002. Both names were concurrently applied until February 2013, when the institution was officially renamed Wuchang District Community Education College. WCEC currently offers programs for degree seekers, adult learners, and youth and seniors in 15 different locations within the district (WCEC, n.d.).

Amalgamation. Community colleges were also built upon amalgamation of two or more institutions (from the same or different sectors of higher education) to amplify educational resources and achieve complementary advantages. This type of community college is a result of reorganization of multiple partners where each contributes to the new institution. For example, Beijing Xicheng Community College (BXCC, *Beijing Xicheng shequ daxue*) was built in the early 2000s through a merger of Xicheng Economic and Scientific University (a 3-year college

NEW DIRECTIONS FOR COMMUNITY COLLEGES • DOI: 10.1002/cc

established in 1986), Xicheng Workers' College (a branch of Beijing RTVU), and Xicheng Workers' Specialized Middle School. It aims to serve the Xicheng District and contributes to its educational and economic development. BXCC currently offers vocational, adult, continuing, and distance education as well as on-the-job training and other types of career training programs. Although the merger was completed almost 15 years ago, the title of the institution still reflects its heritage as Xicheng Economic and Scientific University, and it is jointly listed with its new identity, Xicheng Community College (BXCC, n.d.).

Discussion and Conclusion

The examination of models of community colleges in China as well as their function in the local community reveals that China's education system has actively adapted the U.S. community college concept in postsecondary education institutions. In addition to strengthening vocational colleges and universities, China has developed community colleges as new types of institutions to foster economic and social development with an emphasis on local communities. Although these community colleges have received great attention from the central and local governments, they often face many challenges as they continue emerging in China's higher education system, including struggles between new and old identities, undefined missions in lifelong learning, conflicts among collaborators in restructuring, and balance between global and local needs.

Identity.   It is interesting to note that many community colleges coexist with their heritage institutions, such as RTVUs, vocational colleges, and other types of secondary and postsecondary institutions, from which they were developed or built upon. Lingering on old identities may imply that the community college concept is still not well understood by the Chinese citizens. The term community college may have a negative connotation and might be considered as education of a lower standard, less rigorous, or even not legitimate. Thus, many newly developed community colleges choose, or were forced, to remain connected with the more established component of the institution. For those who finally established community college as their independent identity, the change does not happen overnight. For instance, it took Wuhan Wuchang Community Education College over a decade to be formally recognized as a stand-alone community college. This may explain why many postsecondary vocational colleges and universities are reluctant to include "community college" in their official titles, although they closely resemble the U.S. community college model (Postiglione, 2009). This may indicate that more in-depth discussions need to take place to provide college leaders, administrators, students, and the broader society with a better understanding about the definition of community college as well as its role in China's higher education.

NEW DIRECTIONS FOR COMMUNITY COLLEGES • DOI: 10.1002/cc

Lifelong Learning.   The community colleges discussed in this chapter demonstrate that China has recognized the importance of lifelong education and endeavors to build a learning society through its community college system to provide educational programs suited for every citizen. Although originated following different patterns, these community colleges all provide lifelong learning opportunities and highlight their role in continuing education. China especially relies on RTVUs to establish a network where community colleges can reach out to a wide range of learners, such as rural migrant workers, senior citizens, and laid-off employees (Liu, 2008).

However, community colleges still remain peripheral and have not been identified as official forms of higher education in China. For instance, *Outline of the National Plan for Medium and Long-Term Education Reform and Development (2010–2020)* called for a continuous investment in "accelerating development in further education," "putting further education under a sound framework," "building a flexible, open system for lifelong education," and creating "flyovers" for horizontal and vertical connections among all types of education (2010, pp. 21–22). However, there is no discussion regarding the role that community colleges may play in achieving these goals. To better promote community college development in China and take advantage of this unique educational model, the government needs to clearly define function and responsibilities of these institutions.

Restructuring.   The review of community college models suggests that the Chinese leaders and educators took a pragmatic approach to the development of community colleges. Instead of creating new structures, most of the community colleges were built upon previously established colleges and universities. Many higher education sectors, even secondary schools, were pooled together to form new community colleges. In so doing, community colleges can rely on each partner's strengths and best respond to the local demands; however, they may have to face challenges cooperating with different sectors of higher education. Questions like "how to maximize each partner's strengths," "how to form an administrative team that can provide the most effective leadership," and "how to build a unified identity among different sectors on campus" need to be further investigated.

Local and Global.   The review of the community college examples suggests there is a lack of discussion regarding roles that these institutions may play in a global context. As international education has been steadily growing in China, how community colleges engage in global education while building capacity to advance social and economic development in a local context needs to be addressed. Although Treat and Hagedorn (2013) address their comment to U.S. community colleges only, it rings true to Chinese counterparts as well: "Providing global opportunities with local impact is ... the challenge before all community colleges" (p. 8).

Community education has taken root in China and community colleges will continue evolving and emerging. These institutions have received national and international attention, as they act as major players in

China's education reform, social development, community education, and economic progress. However, it still remains blurry what a community college is in China, where they fit in the current educational system, what models of community colleges have emerged, and whether they function differently in local societies. This chapter touches upon only some major forms of community colleges developed in China. Other models of community colleges, such as those sponsored by private resources, those established independently, and those affiliated with 4-year universities, need to be further investigated. Empirical analysis and in-depth systematic reviews on current community college models would provide meaningful insights into the development of China's community colleges and add new knowledge to adaptation of the U.S. community college model in the world.

References

Beijing Xicheng Community College. (n.d.). *Introduction.* Retrieved from http://www.xcjkd.org/new/news_view.asp?newsid=50, http://www.xcjkd.org:8080/new/news_view.asp?newsid=50

Central People's Government, People's Republic of China. (2014). Li Keqiang: Upgrade "made in China" to "quality manufacturing." Retrieved from http://www.gov.cn/guowuyuan/2014-0

China Central Radio and Television University. (n.d.). *Brief introduction.* Retrieved from http://www.crtvu.edu.cn/topicpage/gaikuang/jianjie.html

Cohen, A. M., Brawer, F. B., & Kisker, C. B. (2014). *The American community college* (6th ed.). San Francisco, CA: Wiley.

Fleishman, S. S., & Luo, Y. (2013). China's top-up policy and the role of community college-like institutions in educational expansion. *Research in Comparative and International Education, 8*(2), 119–131.

Ju, M. (2007). Challenges and strategies of developing workers' colleges. *Vocational Education Research, 3,* 132–133.

Kong, X., & Gimmestad, M. (1999). ERIC Review: U.S. community colleges and China's counterpart institutions. *Community College Review, 27*(3), 77–91.

Liu, Y. (2008). The present situation, problems and countermeasures of community colleges of China. *Fudan Education Forum, 6*(2), 42–47.

Liu, C. (2013). *Study on development of community college in China based on lifelong learning (Doctoral dissertation).* China University of Mining and Technology, Beijing, China.

McBreen, D. P., McBreen, E., & Wu, Z. (1996). China's economic and education reform: A role for community colleges. *Community College Journal of Research and Practice, 20*(3), 253–268. doi:10.1080/1066892960200304

Outline of China's National Plan for Medium and Long-term Education Reform and development (2010–2020). (2010). Retrieved from http://planipolis.iiep.unesco.org/upload/China/China_National_Long_Term_Educational_Reform_Development_2010-2020_eng.pdf

Postiglione, G. A. (2009). Community colleges in China's two systems. In R. L. Raby & E. J. Valeau (Eds.), *Community college models: Globalization and higher education reform* (pp. 157–172). Dordrecht, Netherlands: Springer.

Postiglione, G. A., Wang, J., & Watkins, D. (2015). Vocational and continuing higher education in China. In P. A. Elsner, G. R. Boggs, & J. T. Irwin (Eds.), *Global development*

of community colleges, technical colleges, and further education programs: International research/resource guide (rev. ed., pp. 121–132). Prescott, AZ: Paul Elsner & Associates.
Raby, R. L. (1996). Introduction to part II. In R. L. Raby & N. Tarrow (Eds.), Dimensions of the community college: International, intercultural, and multicultural perspectives (pp. 195–210). New York: Garland.
Raby, R. L. (2009). Chapter 1: Defining the community college model. In R. L. Raby & E. J. Valeau (Eds.), Community college models: Globalization and higher education reform (pp. 3–19). Dordrecht, The Netherlands: Springer.
Roggow, M. J. (2014). The vulnerability of China's vocational colleges: How the global economy is impacting vocational colleges in China. Community College Journal of Research and Practice, 38(8), 748–754. doi:10.1080/10668926.2014.897086
Sun, G. (2005). The action of a community college in construction of the learning community. Journal of Tianjin Adult Higher Learning, 7(1), 12–14.
Tao, B. (2001). Community college in Shanghai. Unpublished presentation at the annual meeting of the American Association of Community Colleges (Chicago, IL, April 5–7, 2001). Retrieved from http://files.eric.ed.gov/fulltext/ED462102.pdf
Treat, T., & Hagedorn, L. S. (2013). Resituating the community college in a global context. In T. Treat & L. S. Hagedorn (Eds.), New Directions for Community Colleges: No. 161. The community college in a global context (pp. 5–9). San Francisco, CA: Jossey-Bass. doi:10.1002/cc.20044
Wei, R. (1997). China's radio & TV universities and the British Open University: A comparative study. Retrieved from http://files.eric.ed.gov/fulltext/ED407601.pdf
Wuchang Community Education College. (n.d.). Introduction. Retrieved from http://www.wcsqjy.com/jieshao/
Yang, R. (2004). Toward massification: Higher education development in the People's Republic of China since 1949. In Higher education: Handbook of theory and research (pp. 311–374). Dordrecht, The Netherlands: Springer.
Yang, Y. (2011). Strengthening development of resources of open universities. Retrieved from http://dianda.china.com.cn/zhuanti/2011-08/26/content_4437594.htm
Zhang, W.-Y., & Shin, N. (2002). Imported or indigenous? A comparative study of three open and distance education models in mainland China, India, and Hong Kong. Open Learning, 17(2), 167–176. doi:10.1080/02680510220146922
Zhejiang RTVU. (n.d.). College review. Retrieved from http://www.zjtvu.edu.cn/xqzl/xxgk.html

Yi (LEAF) Zhang is an assistant professor in the Department of Educational Leadership and Policy Studies at the University of Texas at Arlington.

NEW DIRECTIONS FOR COMMUNITY COLLEGES • DOI: 10.1002/cc

5

This chapter describes the role of career decision-making self-efficacy, academic satisfaction, and institutional support in predicting Korean students' intent to persist in the Academic Credit Bank System.

Persistence of College Students in the South Korean Academic Credit Bank System

Yughi Kim, Kyongsuk Yun

Developed in 1997, the Academic Credit Bank System (ACBS) is a distinctive higher education system in South Korea that enables students to pool credits they earn from various sources toward a degree or plan of study (Usher, 2014). It provides broad access to educational opportunities, allowing students to earn credits and degrees to improve employment outcomes or transition to 4-year institutions. More than 2 million Korean students are currently enrolled in the ACBS, and this number is projected to increase each year (Organisation for Economic Co-operation and Development [OECD], 2009). Enrollment in the ACBS is voluntary and there is no time limit for students to complete their degrees, making it difficult to collect data on student outcomes. Consequently, there is little extant research on the factors that influence ACBS students' persistence toward their educational or career goals. Yet, much like in community colleges in the United States, understanding the factors that prompt ACBS students to stay enrolled can inform policies to benefit their persistence and degree attainment.

Demographic characteristics, such as first-generation college attendance, socioeconomic status, parents' education levels, and academic achievements, predict college student persistence (Schudde & Goldrick-Rab, 2014; Tinto, 1975). Although considering these demographic variables is important, it is also cardinal to assess motivational variables that affect persistence, such as career decision-making self-efficacy (CDMSE), academic satisfaction, and institutional support. To understand the role of these motivational factors in ACBS persistence, this chapter examines

NEW DIRECTIONS FOR COMMUNITY COLLEGES, no. 177, Spring 2017 © 2017 Wiley Periodicals, Inc.
Published online in Wiley Online Library (wileyonlinelibrary.com) • DOI: 10.1002/cc.20241

whether CDMSE, academic satisfaction, and institutional support predict Korean students' intent to persist in the ACBS.

The Academic Credit Bank System

The Academic Credit Bank System was implemented in 1998 in order to recognize diverse learning experiences, including those obtained in and out of school for a high demand for college credentials and work experiences. Various types of institutions within the ACBS include lifelong education centers affiliated with universities, vocational training institutions, and government-affiliated institutions. There are 568 ACBS institutions, serving more than 2,500,000 students across the country (Korean Educational Statistics Service, 2014a, 2014b). The ACBS is distinct from 2-year and 4-year sectors in higher education. The main idea of the ACBS was to provide lifelong learning while promoting opportunities for degree attainment anytime (OECD, 2009). Similar to community colleges in the United States, students with high school degrees or General Educational Development-equivalent qualifications can enroll in the ACBS, accumulate a sufficient number of credits, and then transfer to 4-year institutions to acquire associate's or bachelor's degrees. In addition, because the ACBS institutions offer vocational programs, the ACBS is a particularly attractive option for students as they gain not only academic qualifications but also field experience (OECD, 2009). Given the flexibility of the ACBS, a variety of routes to and through the system are becoming popular, including graduating from high school and immediately participating in the ACBS, transferring to the ACBS from other postsecondary educational institutions, or pausing one's work life to reenroll in the ACBS.

Tinto's (1975) and Bean's (1986) Retention Models

Tinto's (1975) and Bean's (1986) models of student retention helped shape the conceptual framework for this study. These two classic models of student retention theory explain the direct and indirect effects of precollege variables, institutional/goal commitments, and academic and social integration factors on student persistence, given a variety of attributes or precollege experiences and backgrounds. Although Tinto's (1975) model has been criticized by many researchers because it did not account for different student populations, it still provides the significant theoretical framework for student retention studies (Pascarella & Terenzini, 1995). Tinto suggested that dropping out of college could be viewed as a longitudinal process of interactions between the individual and the academic and social systems of the college. Throughout the process, the individual's experiences in these systems continually modify students' goals and institutional commitment, in ways that lead to persistence and/or to varying forms of dropout.

On the other hand, Bean (1986) argued that retention models are similar in structure but differ in the variables assumed to affect retention. Bean's model indicated that the process of attrition depends on the background characteristics of the students. The students interact with the college in organizational, academic, and social aspects; thus, these interactions lead to attitudes that affect students' institutional fit and commitment, which are both potent predictors of continued enrollment. Similarly, grade point average (GPA), which is related to past academic performance and academic integration, has the potential to affect decisions related to continued enrollment. Taken together, these attitudes directly affect students' intentions to stay or leave. Building upon these conceptual frameworks, this chapter reviews the role of students' career decision-making self-efficacy; satisfaction with institution, peers, professors, learning environment, and grades; and institutional support in promoting their intent to persist in the ACBS.

Career Decision-Making Self-Efficacy, Satisfaction, Institutional Role, and Persistence

Previous literature reveals that students who choose their majors and institutions according to their own career goals are highly likely to be engaged in school and to persist. Sandler (2000) discovered that the more confident students are in their ability to make appropriate career-related decisions, the more likely they will persist at college. He concluded that the students with clear career decisions were more likely to remain in the institution. Allen, Robbins, Casillas, and Oh (2008) likewise interviewed college students who chose their majors according to their career interests and found that persistence was directly related to such a choice. Furthermore, students with higher satisfaction levels tend to have higher retention and graduation rates (Miller, 2003, May). Unfortunately, Korean students are often disappointed about their choice of majors once they enter a college (Kim & Kim, 1996). Without prior opportunities to explore their interests, self-efficacy, and goals, they merely write the university entrance exam and enroll in postsecondary institutions according to their grades (Kim & Kim, 1996). By encouraging and motivating students to explore their skills, self-efficacy, and goals, educators can enhance students' satisfaction with institutions and their persistence rates.

Colleges play a critical role in guiding students through their journey to explore career interests, make choices, set goals, and plan the steps to fulfill and persist to their goals. Makela (2011) studied the outcomes of students who participated in individual career counseling and the effectiveness of counseling through students' perspectives; the study proved that students cannot succeed without resources, services, programs, and support provided by their colleges. Indeed, vocational programs should be the place in which students can explore varied career options, are expected to succeed, overcome barriers, and persist.

NEW DIRECTIONS FOR COMMUNITY COLLEGES • DOI: 10.1002/cc

Methodology

This chapter uses quantitative data tracking over 400 students at ACBS vocational training colleges located in Seoul to examine the influence of several factors, including CDMSE, institutional support, and academic satisfaction, on students' intent to persist. In 2013, 500 surveys were distributed to five ACBS institutions located in Seoul. Of the 450 surveys returned, 38 surveys were eliminated due to being incomplete, resulting in 412 survey responses comprising the sample.

The *Career Decision-Making Self-Efficacy Scale* measured the level of individuals' beliefs that they can successfully execute tasks in relation to making career decisions. The survey items on the scale include self-appraisal, collecting career information, goal selection, planning for the future, and problem solving (Betz, Klein, & Taylor, 1996). *Academic satisfaction* is measured with a 19-item survey to understand the importance of attending an institution that fits into students' goals, studying with professors and peers, and being content with one's learning environment, grades, and skills. *Institutional support* refers to the encouragement that instructors, staff, and peers provide students to use the skills and knowledge that they gain from the curriculum, campus culture that promotes continuous learning, support from instructors and peers, and campus culture. Finally, *intent to persist* measures the students' intent to register for classes in the next semester to pursue their education. Items that measured students' intent to persist include the importance of completing a degree, willingness to overcome barriers to persist, motivation to complete an education in the ACBS, and plans to register the next semester. These items were adopted from studies by Kim (2013).

Findings

The sample represented ACBS students attending five colleges in Seoul; 42.7% were females. Among the sampled students, 72% were first-year students and 28% were second-year students. The independent samples t-test results explain that there are differences between male and female students in the degrees of institutional support, academic satisfaction, CDMSE, and intent to persist (see Table 5.1). In fact, male students have significantly higher levels of academic satisfaction, institutional support, CDMSE, and intent to persist than female students. Moreover, the analysis indicated that first-year students have a significantly higher intent to persist than second-year students ($p < .001$). Furthermore, first-year and second-year students do not significantly differ in terms of their academic satisfaction, CDMSE, and perceived institutional support (see Table 5.2).

Intercorrelations among students' CDMSE, academic satisfaction, and perceived institutional support proved that these variables are correlated with their intent to persist (see Table 5.3). Results of ANOVA tests showed a significant difference in the students' intent to persist among the degrees

Table 5.1   T-Test Results Comparing Males and Females on Career Decision-Making Self-Efficacy, Academic Satisfaction, Institutional Support, and Intent to Persist

	Gender	N	Mean	Std. Deviation	Std. Error Mean	t	p-value
Career Decision-Making Self-Efficacy	Male	236	3.3912	.46517	.03028	2.578	0.010[*]
	Female	176	3.2796	.39044	.02943		
Academic Satisfaction	Male	236	3.3874	.54957	.03577	3.437	0.001[***]
	Female	176	3.2001	.54540	.04111		
Institutional Support	Male	236	3.3503	.61479	.04002	3.647	0.000[***]
	Female	176	3.1326	.58752	.04429		
Intent to Persist	Male	236	3.6229	.61152	.03981	2.774	0.006[*]
	Female	176	3.4517	.62567	.04716		

*p < .05, ***p < .001

Table 5.2   T-Test Results Comparing First-Year and Second-Year Students on Career Decision-Making Self-Efficacy, Academic Satisfaction, Institutional Support, and Intent to Persist

	Academic Year	N	Mean	Std. Deviation	Std. Error Mean	t	p-value
Career Decision-Making Self-Efficacy	First-year	297	3.3401	.41595	.02414	-0.241	0.810
	Second-year	115	3.3525	.49169	.04585		
Academic Satisfaction	First-year	297	3.3413	.54082	.03138	1.937	0.054
	Second-year	115	3.2197	.58314	.05438		
Institutional Support	First-year	297	3.2744	.60450	.03508	0.895	0.372
	Second-year	115	3.2130	.63197	.05893		
Intent to Persist	First-year	297	3.6156	.61962	.03595	3.545	0.000[***]
	Second-year	115	3.3797	.60034	.05598		

*p < .05, ***p < .001

of institutional support, students' academic satisfaction, and CDMSE (see Table 5.4). Academic satisfaction had a higher effect on students' intent to persist than CDMSE and institutional support. Students with strong career goals, values, and future plans were more likely to demonstrate an intention to persist than their counterparts with weaker goals, values, and plans. Also, institutional support had a greater impact on students' intent to persist than CDMSE.

NEW DIRECTIONS FOR COMMUNITY COLLEGES • DOI: 10.1002/cc

Table 5.3   Intercorrelations Between Four Variables

Measure		CDMSE	Institutional Support	Academic Satisfaction	Intent to Persist
CDMSE	Pearson Correlation	1	.457**	.440**	.369**
	Sig. (2-tailed)		.000	.000	.000
	N	412	412	412	412
Institutional Support	Pearson Correlation	.457**	1	.651**	.411**
	Sig. (2-tailed)	.000		.000	.000
	N	412	412	412	412
Academic Satisfaction	Pearson Correlation	.440**	.651**	1	.473**
	Sig. (2-tailed)	.000	.000		.000
	N	412	412	412	412
Intent to Persist	Pearson Correlation	.369**	.411**	.473**	1
	Sig. (2-tailed)	.000	.000	.000	
	N	412	412	412	412

$**p < .001$

Table 5.4   ANOVA Tests of Between-Subject Effects

	Sum of Squares	df	Mean Square	F	Sig.
Institutional Support	30.633	18	1.702	5.421	.000***
Academic Satisfaction	32.583	18	1.810	7.569	.000***
CDMSE	14.334	18	.796	4.856	.000***

$*p < .05, ***p < .001$

Discussion

This chapter focused on the influence of students' motivational variables on their intent to persist through the next semester. The findings suggest that first-year male students had a higher level of satisfaction and intention to persist than second-year students or female students. This is inconsistent with findings in the United States, which suggest that female students tend to feel academically and personally supported by faculty and institutions and persist more than do male students (Suhre, Ellen, & Egbert, 2007). The gender differences in the level of satisfaction and intention to persist may result from various factors such as different value systems, confidence levels, behaviors, and aspiration of male and female students (Strayhorn & Saddler, 2009). Future studies must address various variables that result in such gender difference.

Female students showed significantly lower CDMSE, academic satisfaction, and institutional support than male students. Previous literature demonstrates that students' indecisiveness about their careers has a negative impact on school performance (Robertson, Smeets, Lubinski, & Benbow, 2010). Students who were unsure of their career goals and decisions felt less involved with their education and institutions and experienced difficulties in the academic setting. Certainly, if students are accepted into an institution that offers career-related subjects but are unclear as to their career choice, the institution should make efforts to help students explore and develop their career options. Particularly, ACBS faculty and staff should conduct qualitative research to examine the rationale behind female students' low levels of satisfaction, CDMSE, institutional support, and intent to persist.

Results suggest that academic satisfaction had a higher effect on students' intent to persist than CDMSE and institutional support. Students' connectedness with other students and faculty and positive learning experiences are shaped by the collective effort of faculty and students. Students become disengaged in college life when they are discontent with their learning experiences. Indeed, a close relationship between professors and students and a positive impact of institutions on students' career goals, values, and futures are more likely to promote an intention to persist (Deil-Amen, 2011).

Limitations

Several study limitations need to be acknowledged. First, the results of this study are based on data collected by self-reported questionnaires, developed by several researchers. Students' responses may not necessarily reflect their true opinions. For example, because they do not want to look unprepared, the students may respond that they have a higher degree of career decision-making self-efficacy and intention to persist than they actually do. In addition, because the survey questionnaires were originally invented for non-ACBS students, the survey items were not validated on ACBS students. Also, the sample of this study was recruited from five of many institutions in the ACBS. This may narrow the generalizability of the study.

Given the relationship between CDMSE, academic satisfaction, institutional support, and persistence, additional research needs to further investigate these relationships among ACBS students. Follow-up studies should incorporate other student demographic characteristics such as socioeconomic status, high school GPA, and working status. Also, future research should explore the relationship between students' motivational factors and other outcome variables, such as GPA, graduation rates, job placement, and income.

Implications

Despite these limitations, this study makes an important contribution to our knowledge of the relationship between persistence and career decision-making self-efficacy, academic satisfaction, and institutional support among students in South Korea's ACBS. These findings may be especially helpful to inform policy and practice for ACBS faculty members, advisors, policymakers, and educators. In order for college administrators

NEW DIRECTIONS FOR COMMUNITY COLLEGES • DOI: 10.1002/cc

and personnel to better assist their students' academic planning, career development, and persistence, they should consider students' CDMSE and academic satisfaction, as well as the institutional support provided to students. By promoting career service centers, job fairs, or peer advisors, career advisors could guide their students through the process of career searching.

In the United States, three in five traditional-age students (age 24 or under) do not persist in college (National Student Clearinghouse Research Center, 2015). This chapter offers some insight into how credits may be transferred or pooled across different higher education institutions in the United States. Although creating a national system of the ACBS in the United States may require considerable resources and institutional support and research, the ACBS may offer means to avoid credit loss and attrition among students who simultaneously or alternatively attend multiple institutions known as "swirling" (de los Santos & Wright, 1990; Adelman, 2005).

The results of this study also suggest that, as in the United States, Korean student persistence in a specific institution is strongly linked to aligning students' career choices and education plans with their goals and expectations. Advisors in the ACBS institutions provide counseling and advising services to students starting from the first semester. This advising is not limited to academic planning but also includes a personalized process that addresses students' interests, goals, and personal characteristics. In addition, advisors in the ACBS are typically professors who have expertise in certain disciplinary areas. This takes advantage of professors' expertise in academic planning that fits students' interests, goals, and motivations.

Furthermore, ACBS institutions offer work-study programs, internships, and career services so students can consider various career options and establish career goals. In fact, college students often face difficulties regarding career choices and encounter career barriers along their paths. Previous studies show that traditional-age students, who are least likely to have had a career prior to their enrollment in college, are greatly influenced by their colleges and communities when they make career goals. Based on this assertion, it is essential that colleges develop adequate programs and strategies to assist students in exploring a wide range of career options (Makela, 2011).

Guiding students to explore different academic majors and related interests may help them to develop an academic or a career goal. This type of institutional support may enhance students' satisfaction with institutions and their intent to persist. Students choose their majors for various reasons. They may do so to please their parents, to be with their peers, or to ease the anxiety of being undecided. Students could interact with faculty, advisors, and peers to help them understand the relationship between their major and career options. Guiding students to the right path for them is not solely the advisor's or counselor's task. Such opportunities should be integrated into campus life, course content, and faculty–student interaction. For instance, professors who integrate real-life lessons into course content or give their students opportunities to consider their values, interests, and goals during the course may be great benefit to students' success. Having a goal, indeed, will motivate and encourage students to pursue their academics.

References

Allen, J., Robbins, S. B., Casillas, A., & Oh, I. S. (2008). Third-year college retention and transfer: Effects of academic performance, motivation, and social connectedness. *Research in Higher Education, 49*(7), 647–664.

Adelman, C. (2005). *Moving into town and moving one. The community college in the lives of traditional-age students.* Washington, DC: National Center for Education Statistics.

Bean, J. P. (1986). Assessing and reducing attrition. In D. Hossler (Ed.), *New Directions for Higher Education: No. 53. Managing College Environments* (pp. 47–61). San Francisco, CA: Jossey-Bass. doi:10.1002/he.36919865306

Betz, N. E., Klein, K. L., & Taylor, K. M. (1996). Evaluation of a short form of the career decision-making self-efficacy scale. *Journal of Career Assessment, 4*(1), 47–57.

Deil-Amen, R. (2011). Socio-academic integrative moments: Rethinking academic and social integration among two-year college students in career-related programs. *The Journal of Higher Education, 82*(1), 54–91.

de los Santos Jr, A., & Wright, I. (1990). Maricopa's swirling students: Earning one-third of Arizona state's bachelor's degrees. *Community, Technical, and Junior College Journal, 60*(6), 32–34.

Kim, H. J. (2013). *Cyberdaehaksengeui Jagihyoneunggam, Hakseupjeonryak Hwalyong Sujoon, Hakupsojin, Hakgyojiwoneh Ddarun Gwamok Manjokdo Mit Hakupjisokeuihyang Yaechuk* [Predicting the cyber students' satisfaction by examining self- efficacy, practical use of study strategies, academic exhaustion, and institution support] (Unpublished master's thesis). Ewha Women's University, Seoul, South Korea.

Kim, K. H., & Kim, B. W. (1996). *Cognitive and behavioral aspects in the career development of Korean college students.*

Korean Educational Statistics Service. (2014a). Education & training institutions by type. Retrieved from http://kess.kedi.re.kr/eng/index

Korean Educational Statistics Service. (2014b). Enrollments by types of institutions. Retrieved from http://kess.kedi.re.kr/eng/index

Makela, J. P. (2011). *Career counseling as an environmental support: Exploring influences on career choice, career decision-making self-efficacy, and career barriers (Doctoral dissertation).* University of Illinois, Champaign-Urbana.

Miller, R. (2003, May). *Student satisfaction and institutional success.* Paper presented at the 43rd annual AIR Forum, Tampa, FL.

National Student Clearinghouse Research Center. (2015). Completing college: A national view of student attainment rates-fall 2009 cohort. Retrieved from https://nscresearchcenter.org/signaturereport10/

Organisation for Economic Co-operation and Development. (2009). *Recognition of non-formal and informal learning.* Country note for Korea. Paris, France: Author.

Pascarella, E. T., & Terenzini, P. T. (1995). The impact of college on students: Myths, rational myths, and some other things that may not be true. *NACADA Journal, 15*(2), 26–33.

Robertson, K. F., Smeets, S., Lubinski, D., & Benbow, C. P. (2010). Beyond the threshold hypothesis even among the gifted and top math/science graduate students, cognitive abilities, vocational interests, and lifestyle preferences matter for career choice, performance, and persistence. *Current Directions in Psychological Science, 19*(6), 346–351.

Sandler, M. E. (2000). Career decision-making self-efficacy, perceived stress, and an integrated model of student persistence: A structural model of finances, attitudes, behavior, and career development. *Research in Higher Education, 41*(5), 537–580.

Schudde, L., & Goldrick-Rab, S. (2014). On second chances and stratification how sociologists think about community colleges. *Community College Review, 43*(1), 27–45.

Strayhorn, T. L., & Saddler, T. N. (2009). Gender differences in the influence of faculty–student mentoring relationships on satisfaction with college among African Americans. *Journal of African American Studies, 13*(4), 476–493.

Suhre, C. J., Jansen, E. P., & Harskamp, E. G. (2007). Impact of degree program satisfaction on the persistence of college students. *Higher Education, 54*(2), 207–226.

Usher, A. (2014). *The korean academic credit bank: A model for credit transfer in north america?* Toronto: Higher Education Strategy Associates.

YUGHI KIM *is a doctoral student in the Program in Higher Education Leadership at the University of Texas at Austin.*

KYONGSUK YUN *is president of Corea Culinary Officer Occupational Training College in Seoul, South Korea.*

NEW DIRECTIONS FOR COMMUNITY COLLEGES • DOI: 10.1002/cc

6

This chapter describes the multifaceted history and future trajectory of community colleges in India and considers implications for policy and practice.

Understanding Community Colleges in the Indian Context

Jillian L. Gross

India will soon have the largest and youngest population in the world, yet less than 20% of 15- to 29-year-olds enroll in postsecondary education (Ministry of Human Resource Development [MHRD], 2014). Those who are able to enroll face challenges of quality and relevance in a highly political, largely privatized, and acutely rigid education system (Tilak, 2013). Furthermore, for those who earn a credential, only 15% are considered employable (Singh, 2012). In an attempt to reform the elite higher education system, policymakers and practitioners promote community colleges as an ideal solution to address issues of access and equity plaguing India's postsecondary education (Agarwal, 2009). Since 1995, community colleges have spread to every state in the country. Yet, leaders are struggling to establish a sustainable development model because of the effort required to challenge the status quo of an elite, theory-based higher education system.

To date, Indian community colleges (ICCs), framed as "education for employment," have developed in three overlapping phases: first, a nongovernmental organizational (NGO) model operating on the periphery of formal education; second, national expansion through the open education system; and third, incorporation in formal higher and technical education institutions. All share the professed goal of disrupting an inequitable educational system and conform to the globalized concept of a community college by offering flexible postsecondary education to underserved students in a local context (Raby & Valeau, 2012). Yet, ICCs vary widely in form and function within and between phases. This chapter is intended to serve as an introduction to the complex landscape of ICCs and is based on interviews with Indian policymakers, practitioners, and ICC leaders conducted throughout 2015.

New Directions for Community Colleges, no. 177, Spring 2017 © 2017 Wiley Periodicals, Inc.
Published online in Wiley Online Library (wileyonlinelibrary.com) • DOI: 10.1002/cc.20242

Postsecondary Education in India

Organized postsecondary education in India is the legacy of an elite exam-based system implemented during British rule now encompassing a rigid and hierarchical four-stream structure that includes higher, technical, vocational, and open/distance education. Only 12% of students in India complete 12 years of schooling, and there is a 50% attrition rate at each year of secondary education (MHRD, 2014). Overall, persistent challenges vexing the system include high dropout rates; inequality of opportunity based on geography, gender, caste/tribe, socioeconomic status, and religion; and general quality of education (Carnoy & Dossani, 2013; Tilak, 2013).

Students, parents, and employers often view any credential other than a degree, especially those earned in an industrial training institute or polytechnic, as "second class" in a society that generally views skilled trades as low-status employment (Singh, 2012). Socially and economically marginalized students predominantly pursue these credentials, which critics regularly argue are outdated, low-quality education that rarely leads to sustainable employment (King, 2012). In order to address these inequities, the central government recently began shifting education reform priorities from mere expansion to focus on quality, employability, and accountability (Carnoy & Dossani, 2013; Tilak, 2013).

Guiding this work is a massive "skilling" campaign that pledges to "bridge the social, regional, gender, and economic divide" (Ministry of Finance, 2013. This quote comes from a 2013 press release online that is less than one page. Retrieved from http://pib.nic.in/newsite/mbErel.aspx?relid =96468) and provide both vertical and horizontal mobility within and between education, training, and the labor market (Ministry of Skill Development and Entrepreneurship [MSDE], 2015). In an attempt to standardize and coordinate activities, a competency-based *National Skills Qualification Framework* (NSQF) is in the early stages of implementation. This is the first concentrated national push to "vocationalize" education and focus on increasing the employability of students through higher education (MSDE, 2015). Postsecondary education institutions, motivated by substantial funding opportunities, are beginning to offer new courses aligned with the framework. Higher education officials have even inaugurated modular pathways from ICC through a PhD under the framework; but it is too early to assess how well these programs fulfill the promise of flexibility, mobility, and improved employment prospects.

Community Colleges in India

The idea of developing a system of junior colleges in India dates back to the 1930s (Odgers, 1933), but these were envisioned to serve as a bridge between lower secondary school and university in the years before compulsory secondary school. It was not until a delegate from the new College of Vocational Studies at the University of Delhi attended the Wingspread

Conference on International Education and the Community College in 1978 that education reformers began considering the adaptation of the community college model in India (Yarrington, 1978). It would be more than a decade before the idea began to flourish.

In 1995, Pondicherry University established the country's first community college (Singh, 2012); and Madras Community College, the first NGO ICC, followed in 1996. Although existing institutions such as polytechnics and industrial training institutes also conform to the globalized concept of a community college (Raby & Valeau, 2012), their terminal curricula and disconnection from the local context left stakeholders seeking an alternative approach (Anand & Polite, 2010). Therefore, early ICCs were actively promoted as being based on the North American model but "adjusted to meet India's unique needs and aspirations" (Alphonse, 2013, p. 17).

By 1998, Dr. Xavier Alphonse, a Jesuit priest and university administrator, established the Indian Centre for Research and Development of Community Education (ICRDCE) in Tamil Nadu. Over the last 20 years, Alphonse has arguably been the single most influential actor in the growth of ICCs. Through workshops, teacher training programs, and consultations with policymakers, ICRDCE promotes ICCs as a solution to an ailing educational system that largely ignores marginalized students (Alphonse, 2013). Under his leadership, ICRDCE developed hands-on and personal development-oriented curricula that diverged significantly from the heavily theory-based curricula of conventional education in India. With ICRDCE helping establish over 300 ICCs in 25 states and steering national ICC policy design (ICRDCE, 2015), the concept gained traction at the state and national levels.

Encouraged by ICRDCE, in 2008, the Tamil Nadu state government adopted progressive policies to promote ICCs (Alphonse 2013). Subsequently, Tamil Nadu Open University has recognized 204 community colleges, and many traditional colleges and universities began establishing NGO ICCs. NGO ICCs largely offer short-term certificate and diploma programs for students without the ability to transfer into degree programs, whereas Open University ICCs are designed to allow vertical mobility within Tamil Nadu Open University only.

Building on the momentum in South India, Alphonse led efforts to establish national recognition for ICCs—the second phase of development. In 2009, after years of advocacy, Indira Gandhi National Open University (IGNOU) established a community college initiative that allowed organizations "rooted in community-based activities" to register as an ICC (IGNOU, 2011, p. 14). The IGNOU policy outlined a curriculum of stackable credentials with the possibility of transfer into an IGNOU degree program (IGNOU, 2011). Within the first 3 years, IGNOU registered over 600 ICCs, many of which were already associated with ICRDCE. IGNOU's network model offered ICCs national recognition without being constrained by the conventional postsecondary education system; but quick expansion without the necessary infrastructure in place left the new program vulnerable.

Almost as quickly as IGNOU ICCs opened, the initiative was discontinued. Despite attempts to monitor the new ICCs, by spring 2012, IGNOU's board of management suspended the program due to a lack of oversight and quality assurance. Two subsequent review committees concluded that the ICCs should continue but would need more rigorous accountability measures. Despite these findings, the board of management, under the leadership of a new vice chancellor, unexpectedly issued a letter discontinuing all IGNOU ICCs as of July 2013. There was legal and political backlash from students and ICCs for this decision and many credentials are yet to be issued.

Simultaneous to the rise and fall of the IGNOU scheme, the central government was planning to expand ICCs into higher and technical education. National planning documents began including the ICC concept as early as 2002, but it was not until the most recent strategic plan (2012–2017) that the Planning Commission (2011) explicitly called for the integration of existing ICCs and the expansion of a multifaceted system "based on the North American Model." Inaugurating the third phase of ICC development, the colleges were to "provide modular credit-based courses with entry and exit flexibility that conforms to the National Skills Qualification Framework" (p. 101).

Hence, the Ministry of Human Resource Development initiated a parallel ICC initiative to be housed within traditional colleges, universities, and polytechnics. ICRDCE and a new prominent player, the Wadhwani Foundation—a Bangalore-based NGO—provided official support. The ministry began funding its new ICCs in late 2013, after years of deliberation, collaboration, and mobilization of policymakers, industry partners, academics, and international collaborators. Seventy-two polytechnics and 64 traditional colleges and universities received funding that year. Rather than creating stand-alone institutions, new ICCs operate much like a small department within an institution, offering new skill-based vocational education credentials in high-growth industries (Suraksha, 2015). With the central government's new prioritization of skill development and educational reform, national efforts to standardize and regulate ICCs began.

ICCs Today.   To date, there is no centralized database to register ICCs from different founding contexts. This makes it impossible to pinpoint the exact number of ICCs given wide variance in definition and implementation; existence of independent ICCs with no affiliation to ICRDCE, IGNOU, or the central government; and overlap in ICCs between each phase of growth. This leaves most ICCs operating independently with little interorganizational awareness or communication and minimal oversight or accountability.

As of January 2016, over 200 ICCs associate formally with ICRDCE, which helped establish and monitor many more (ICRDCE, 2015). ICRDCE is encouraging curricular alignment with the *National Skills Qualification Framework*, while continuing to promote an NGO ICC model (X. Alphonse, personal communication [The three "personal communication" citations are from interviews I conducted with individuals. I included citations because I did not write the chapter as a research paper. That being said, rather than cite as "personal communication," I would prefer to remove all four citations as is standard with a qualitative research study to protect the confidentiality of my research participants. Father Xavier was the only one who was comfortable with his name being used]). IGNOU is in the process of formalizing a new scheme to align with the framework and multiple states run ICCs through their state Open University system. Additionally, many former IGNOU ICCs continue their operations autonomously, without official recognition for their programs.

In the third-phase of ICCs initiated by the Ministry of Human Resource Development as of November 2015, the University Grants Commission (UGC) had conducted three selection processes and partially funded more than 200 ICCs in colleges and universities. In addition to the initial 72 ICCs funded at polytechnics, in 2014, the All India Council on Technical Education gave each of its 3,500 institutions an unfunded mandate to train at least 100 students per year under the framework. As the council defines a community college as any technical institution offering at least one course aligned with the framework (Mantha, 2014), this policy effectively renders all of its institutions ICCs, in name if not in practice. As of November 2015, higher and technical education officials were hopeful about the future of ICCS, but funding and political support remain tenuous.

Implementation of the framework, and its centralized oversight by the new Ministry of Skill Development and Entrepreneurship, provides a mechanism for potential convergence among different types of ICCs. Currently, the promise of educational mobility, although thoughtfully incorporated into policy design, is largely unrealized in practice. ICC norms and expectations are generally shared through one-way communications—workshops and the distribution of guidelines—from ICRDCE, IGNOU, and now central government agencies. Generally, there is no meaningful opportunity for feedback, sustained interorganizational activity, or ongoing oversight to ensure consistency or cohesion in implementation. Furthermore, future funding, and therefore the viability of ICCs, is in jeopardy. In light of these opportunities and challenges, ICCs are well positioned to serve as a catalyst for educational, economic, and social reform; but their ultimate form, function, and position within postsecondary education remain uncertain.

Making Sense of the ICC Landscape

The key to ICC growth rests in simultaneous strategies to secure local interest alongside regional and national policy support among leaders. Despite the interconnection of these actors, there is no formal feedback mechanism that allows practice to inform policy; no meaningful oversight; and inconsistent expectations among ICC phases. Although Indian community colleges universally offer skill development education to marginalized students, community college practitioners themselves rarely interact. Instead, the concept is largely spread through mandatory workshops rather than professional networks, and participation is stimulated by the lure of government-controlled recognition. Operating in relative isolation, college leaders have wide latitude to interpret the concept in practice, leaving implementation fragmented. Course structure and content, eligibility criteria among students, and mobility within postsecondary education and employment are inconsistent among ICCs. Although leaders work to legitimize community colleges at the national level, their efforts are unlikely to ensure organizational viability if policy remains disconnected from practice.

By all anecdotal accounts, the ingredients for ICC success include a leadership team committed to the individual needs of students, faculty committed to nonconventional curricula and teaching methodologies, industry partners committed to providing a high-quality educational experience for students, and students committed to personal development. The result of these commitments, when firmly rooted in the local community, is an equitable partnership that helps students pursue further education and secure sustainable employment with realistic possibilities for upward mobility and lifelong learning. However, ensuring these conditions is no easy task.

The danger of such an intentionally vocational focus, as Brint and Karabel (1989) concluded about U.S. community colleges, lies in the potential for ICCs to serve as a tool to reproduce, rather than ameliorate, social inequalities. In India, this concern is exacerbated by a complex social context informed by an ancient history of caste and a modern history of colonialism. The current reality includes extreme economic disparities, lack of educational opportunity, and a largely unorganized labor market in the world's most populous democracy. Tilak (2013) argues, "The massive program [i.e., skilling] is being planned not as a part of secondary or higher education, but effectively as another tier in the education system that can facilitate segregation of the students into vocational education and higher education" (p. 42). That being said, vocationalization, if aligned with the needs and aspirations of youth over and above the needs of the economy, could help reform a rigid and bureaucratic educational system into a more engaging, inclusive, and equitable experience. Such an effort would make great strides toward enhancing the "social acceptability" of (nonengineering) technical and vocational education.

Because the state alone controls educational certification in India, to secure credibility, ICCs contort themselves to align with a revolving set of government policies that are set with little regard for local implementation. This gives the state significant power over what it means to be an ICC conceptually, but little power over what it means in practice. For example, all ICCs maintain adherence to a norm of employment education, but its enactment varies based on founding context and organizational leadership. As ICC control has shifted from grassroots efforts to state-organized initiatives, the priority of national economic development has begun to overshadow the early goals of student development at the system level. Yet, practitioners at the organizational level have nearly free reign to interpret the concept to satisfy their personal interests, which may complement or compete with changing expectations related to government recognition. Because assessment and funding plans can dramatically shape implementation, how future policies are crafted will be critical to achieving educational justice and the ultimate success or failure of ICCs.

Considerations for Policy and Practice

According to Indian policymakers and practitioners, aligning education to employment and implementing experiential pedagogies require a change in mindset and practice that cannot be achieved overnight. Transitioning from textbook-based exams to competency-based evaluations demands new learning methods that have been largely absent from postsecondary education. It cannot be overstated that the teachers, trainers, and industry partners being asked to implement new skills-based vocational education are themselves the products of the conventional education system. Therefore, increased attention to *how* teachers and trainers are prepared to accomplish this new work is imperative (Goel, 2015).

Rather than top-down information dissemination, professional development designed to engage participants in collective knowledge sharing could provide valuable opportunities to identify common challenges and opportunities, share problem-solving techniques, and foster postmeeting interaction. Such activities could help develop support structures and create professional standards that reflect the experience of the grassroots level in order to buffer ICCs from an ever-changing parade of policymakers who often have little expertise in education. This conclusion reflects anecdotal evidence from ICC stakeholders and my experience witnessing the power of (relatively rare) opportunities for interaction between ICC leaders. Without the reinforcement of local practitioners, the ICCs' potentially transformative educational approach may wither.

Practitioners generally agree that the most successful implementation of skills courses in ICCs has been the result of dedicated educators putting the individual transformation of students at the core of their work. This means that more than providing employability skills, effective practitioners at the grassroots level are focusing on the holistic development of "responsible citizens" (former IGNOU Vice Chancellor Pillai quoted in Anand & Polite, 2010, p. 15). In light of this success, prioritizing individual transformation over workforce transformation in future policy and practice could help ensure social justice outcomes rather than the reproduction of an elite system.

Complementary to prioritizing student development, viewing the framework as a baseline to be augmented and adapted in the local context will be imperative. In a country as diverse as India, only a local focus is likely to provide the necessary fit between employer expectations, student learning, and entrepreneurship opportunities. This will help ensure sustainable employment for students with the possibility of upward mobility while providing incentives to employers to hire trained individuals for higher initial wages—primary concerns among skill development leaders.

A final caveat: India is an increasingly attractive site for U.S. community college involvement and both countries prioritize bilateral collaboration. Some examples include the Obama–Singh Knowledge initiative and the U.S.–India Higher Education Dialogues, the United States India Educational Foundation, and numerous U.S. community colleges that have forged independent partnerships across India. In 2013, the American Association of Community Colleges signed a memorandum of understanding (MOU) with the All India Council for Technical Education to support ICC development. Despite concerted efforts from both partners including multiple site visits, this MOU has seen very little progress. To date, differing expectations over funding, institutional selection, and authority to implement, among other challenges, have created seemingly insurmountable roadblocks.

Partnership is often challenging because of differing expectations born out of the vastly different systems. India has a highly centralized system that treats higher, technical, vocational, and open/distance education as distinct streams of postsecondary education with regulated by different agencies along with a nascent and largely voluntary accreditation system. On the other hand, U.S. higher education is a largely decentralized system marked by organizational autonomy, a well-developed accreditation scheme, and a comprehensive approach to postsecondary education. The scale and speed of change possible within each system or within a given institution are markedly different as is the ability to mandate participation (or not). All collaborations should carefully consider contextual differences in a highly political environment. Partnership is likely to be stymied without understanding systematic differences and working to find common ground from which to begin operating. This work requires deep wells of patience, perseverance, and a willingness to learn from each other as much as teach.

Conclusion

Because practitioners are isolated, accountability is negligible, and policy decisions are based on anecdotal evidence rather than professional expertise, ICCs are in danger of falling victim to the fickle winds of political and economic change. Yet, powerful reform would be possible with policy design that stimulates knowledge sharing, creates substantive feedback mechanisms, and buffers practitioners from short-term policy and funding concerns. Therefore, the experience of leaders working every day to legitimize ICCs and bring coherence to a disjointed system should be used to elevate the often-silenced voice of practitioners in future policy initiatives. Only by bridging the divide between policy and practice will enable ICCs fulfill their promise as a meaningful gateway to postsecondary education and employment.

References

Agarwal, P. (2009). *Indian higher education: Envisioning the future.* Mumbai, India: Sage Publications.

Alphonse, X. A. (2013). The Indian community college system: Inspiration from community colleges in the United States. In N. Jha (Ed.), *The U.S. community college model: Potential for applications in India* (pp. 17–22). New Delhi, India: Institute for International Education.

Anand, N., & Polite, S. (2010). Looking for answers. *EDU Tech for Leaders in Higher Education, 1*(7), 10–17.

Brint, S., & Karabel, J. (1989). *The diverted dream: Community colleges and the promise of educational opportunity in America,* 1900–1985. New York, NY: Oxford University Press.

Carnoy, M., & Dossani, R. (2013). Goals and governance of higher education in India. *Higher Education, 65*(5), 595–612.

Goel, A. (2015, July). Seven pillars for national skills policy. *Human Capital Magazine.* Retrieved from http://wadhwani-foundation.org/press/seven-pillars-for-national-skills-policy-ajay-goel-featured-in-human-capital-magazine/

Indian Center for Research and Development of Community Education. (2015, July 15). *Role of ICRDCE.* Retrieved from http://www.icrdce.com/roleoficrdce.html

Indira Gandhi National Open University. (2011). *Guidelines for community colleges.* New Delhi, India: Indira Gandhi National Open University.

King, K. (2012). The geopolitics and meanings of India's massive skills development ambitions. *International Journal of Educational Development, 32*(5), 665–673.

Mantha, S. S. (2014). National skills qualification framework (NSQF), credit framework, regulations and faculty qualifications [PowerPoint slides]. Retrieved from http://www.knowyourcollege-gov.in/resources/workshop_ppt/Output/37-SS%20MANTHA_Skills_051214.ppsx

Ministry of Finance. (2013). *Government sets-up the national skill development agency.* New Delhi, India: Press Information Bureau, Government of India.

Ministry of Human Resource Development. (2014). *Annual report* 2013–14. New Delhi, India: Government of India.

Ministry of Skill Development and Entrepreneurship. (2015). *National policy for skill development and entrepreneurship* 2015. New Delhi, India: Government of India. Retrieved from http://pibphoto.nic.in/documents/rlink/2015/jul/p201571503.pdf

Odgers, G. A. (1933). A junior college movement in India. *Junior College Journal, 4*(1), 3–7.

Planning Commission, Government of India. (2011). *Twelfth five year plan* (2012–2017). New Delhi, India: Sage Publications.

Raby, R. L., & Valeau, E. J. (2012). Educational borrowing and the emergence of community college global counterparts. *International Perspectives on Education and Society, 17,* 19–46.

Singh, M. (2012). India's national skills development policy and implications for TVET and lifelong learning. In M. Pilz (Ed.), *The future of vocational education and training in a changing world* (pp. 179–211). Wiesbaden, Germany: Springer.

Suraksha, P. (2015, February). A study on skilling. *New Indian Express*. Retrieved from http://www.newindianexpress.com/education/edex/A-Study-on-Skilling/2015/02/16/article2665935.ece

Tilak, J. B. G. (2013). India: Reforming education in the neo liberal era. In Y. Wang (Ed.), *Education policy reform trends in G20 members* (pp. 33–53). Berlin, Germany: Springer.

Yarrington, R. (1978). *Internationalizing community colleges. Report of a Wingspread Conference*. Washington, DC: American Association of Community and Junior Colleges.

JILLIAN LEIGH GROSS *is a doctoral candidate at the University of Michigan, Ann Arbor, in the Center for the Study of Higher and Postsecondary Education.*

Since the end of apartheid, South African leaders have been working to transform all aspects of the racialized society into a nonracialized, nonsexist democratic state, including postsecondary education. This chapter examines the changing South African collegiate context focusing on access, persistence, affordability, accreditation, transfer, and future trends.

7

South African Universities Viewed Through a Community College Lens

Kristin Bailey Wilson, Wouter Van Alebeek

Since the passage of the 1996 Constitution of the Republic of South Africa, the government leaders have been working to transform all aspects of the racialized, apartheid society into a nonracialized, nonsexist democratic state. This work includes government, the economy, health care, infrastructure, judicial, primary and secondary education, and higher education. In 1997, the Higher Education Act (HEA) was passed and formed the basis for transforming the educational system. The South African Qualifications Authority (SAQA) was charged with instituting the National Qualifications Framework, a 10-level matrix describing the type of learning to occur from primary to doctoral levels. In addition, the HEA gave the Department of Higher Education and Training (DHET) the power to merge public institutions to achieve greater diversity in the student body (Ministry of Education, 2001). Between 2002 and 2005, institutions were merged to form comprehensive universities, and in 2013, two new universities of technology were formed. The resultant landscape is made up of 11 traditional universities, 6 comprehensive universities, and 8 technical universities. Comprehensive universities have the most in common with American community colleges in that they offer both general education (or academic programs) and technical programs. However, students can earn bachelor's, master's, and doctoral degrees at comprehensive universities.

Despite the mergers and policy changes, students have actively complained about teaching languages (Afrikaans vs. English), fees, outsourcing, and campus monuments. October 2015 will not be forgotten by college leaders or students. Starting with the University of Witwatersrand,

NEW DIRECTIONS FOR COMMUNITY COLLEGES, no. 177, Spring 2017 © 2017 Wiley Periodicals, Inc.
Published online in Wiley Online Library (wileyonlinelibrary.com) • DOI: 10.1002/cc.20243

colleges throughout the country have experienced protests that have cancelled classes, destroyed property, and delayed normal operations. Nelson Mandela Metropolitan University was forced to cancel a ceremony for honors students when protesters took over the venue for the event. At the University of Western Cape, Cape Peninsula University of Technology, and the University of Fort Hare protests forced campus lockdowns as well as costing millions of dollars in damage. When more than 10,000 protestors converged in Pretoria at the Union Building (seat of government), President Jacob Zuma agreed to cancel plans to increase university fees and to appoint a committee to look into the problem of funding. This protest movement is shaping the landscape of higher education even as we write this chapter. As registration began for the 2016 year, protestors at the University of Witwatersrand and the University of Johannesburg disrupted campuses to protest the payment of fees and are advocating free college. Campus leaders at the University of Johannesburg encouraged students to enroll online to avoid protesters on campus. No institutional type or geographical location has been immune to protests. Although the United States has not experienced widespread protests concerning the cost of college, many national and state politicians have campaigned on the promise of free community college without solving the question of how campus leaders are to offer a growing curricular and student services infrastructure to students who are attending for free; in states with decreasing commitments to college funding; and in a nation that contends education is a state responsibility. Campus leaders in South Africa and in the United States have much in common in this regard.

Therefore, this chapter examines postsecondary education in South Africa using mission concerns that are emblematic of American community colleges: access, affordability, accreditation, transfer, and persistence.

Access

Increasing enrollment of Black, Indian, and mixed-race students was central to the transformation of South African higher education. From 2000 to 2012, universities had a 71% increase in headcount enrollment. Comprehensive universities have experienced the largest growth, a 84% increase, whereas universities of technology have experienced the least, a 39% increase (Higher Education Management Information System [HEMIS], 2012). As with the United States, institutional type matters. South African students are voting with their feet and demonstrating a preference for academic programs rather than technical ones. Of the comprehensive universities, the University of South Africa (UNISA) has the largest enrollment at 336,300 students in 2012. UNISA is largely online and distance education offering both technical and academic degrees, including doctoral degrees. UNISA enrolls 35% of all college students in South Africa. Figure 7.1 shows head count enrollment in thousands for the three institutional types.

Figure 7.1. Head Count Enrollment in the 1,000s.
Data Are Not Available for the Two New Universities of Technology:
University of Mpumalanga and Sol Plaatje University.

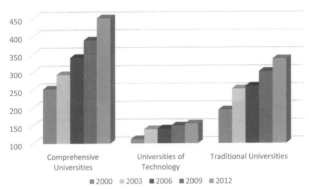

Source: HEMIS, 2012.

Figure 7.2. Black Participation at Comprehensive Universities

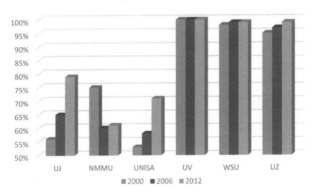

Source: HEMIS, 2012.

The transformation of higher education is premised on the notion that the postsecondary infrastructure was highly racialized and needed to be more balanced. In 1993, 71% of Whites attended college after their secondary education, whereas only 9% of Blacks attended (Menon, 2015). By 2011, 59% of Whites were attending college, whereas Black participation had increased to 12%. However, the increase falls disproportionately with UNISA. Figure 7.2 shows Black enrollment percentages at each of the comprehensive universities: University of Johannesburg (UJ), Nelson Mandela Metropolitan University (NMMU), University of South Africa (UNISA), University of Venda (UV), Walter Sisulu University (WSU) and University of Zululand (UZ). At universities of technology, Black participation ranged from 55% to 98% in 2012.

NEW DIRECTIONS FOR COMMUNITY COLLEGES • DOI: 10.1002/cc

Although Blacks make up the majority of students enrolled, the national plan is for enrollment in postsecondary education to mirror race percentages in the total population (Gyimah-Brempong & Ondiege, 2011). Eighty percent of South Africa's population is Black. Soudien (2010) estimated that only 12% of eligible Black South Africans enroll in postsecondary education. The student participation rate for adults between the ages of 20 and 24 is around 18%; in the United States, it is 40%. For adults between 18 and 19, the South African participation rate is 12%, whereas the U.S. participation rate is 71% (Menon, 2015; U.S. Department of Education, 2012). Although policy changes and funding have changed the landscape of higher education in South Africa, they still have a long way to go to meet their transformation goals.

A review report issued by the Council on Higher Education (CHE, 2016) described the various efforts to increase Black and Colored participation in college, including merging racially segregated institutions; changing admissions requirements; developing the National Qualifications Framework (NQF) to ensure the quality of curricular offerings from preschool to doctoral level; discouraging language discrimination by requiring that lectures be offered in English, as opposed to Afrikaans; the development of the National Student Financial Aid Scheme; and building new universities in underserved areas. Although all of these efforts have helped, they have also upended the stable higher education landscape in higher education and resulted in a myriad of unintended consequences (e.g., the #OpenStellenbosch social media campaign). The efforts have also made clear the substantial gap in the national funding available for college infrastructure development and the real need for resources (CHE, 2016).

Persistence

Despite the changes in admissions standards, the merging of institutions, the changing of funding structures, and policy developments galore, college students struggle to persist to degree attainment. South African scholars have begun to ask access to what? For every 100 Black students who begin postsecondary education, only 5 graduate (Soudien, 2010). Collins and Millard (2013) noted that the most pressing challenge in higher education is to understand why completion rates are so low for particular groups and to make the institutional transformations necessary to support these groups. College diplomas are similar to an associate's degree in that they are in a particular subject and often focused on technical learning. Figure 7.3 shows dropout rates by year and in total for diplomas and undergraduate degrees.

The total dropout rate in 2012 for students intending to earn a diploma was 56% and for students intending to earn an undergraduate degree was 46%. The other vantage point for student persistence is to

Figure 7.3.   Dropout Rates for Diplomas and Undergraduate Degrees

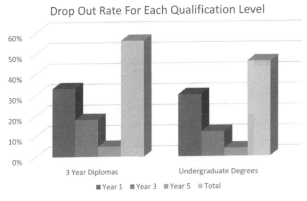

Source: HEMIS, 2012.

Figure 7.4.   Graduates as a Percentage of Head Count at Comprehensive Universities

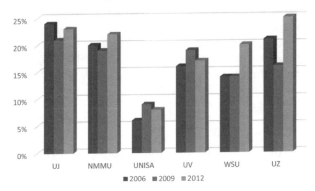

Source: HEMIS, 2012.

look at graduation rates. Figure 7.4 presents graduates as a percentage of head count for comprehensive universities. The most serious challenges to persistence appear to be preparedness, affordability, and living expenses. Preparedness and living expenses are discussed in this section, and affordability is discussed in detail in the following section.

In order to graduate from high school, students must take an exam and earn the National Senior Certificate. The certificate is commonly called matriculation or matric. Scoring well on the matric means college admission. In 2015, the pass rate to earn the National Senior Certification dropped from 76% to 71%. The rural provinces performed far worse than did the more urban areas. Although this seems like bad news, there was a 14% increase in the number of test takers. The underlying positive may be that more students are seeing a high school education as important for employment and postsecondary education. Nonetheless, focusing on the quality of secondary education in rural areas is critical to improving postsecondary persistence.

In addition to a lack of preparedness, college students in South Africa struggle to find adequate housing and food. Although comprehensive data on living conditions of students is not collected, so it is not possible to quantify the problem, a 2012 report by the Department of Higher Education and Training (DHET, 2012) found that Black, female, and first-year students are the primary victims of inadequate accommodations and food. The report said that some students are "starving" and that the living conditions are "squalid." The report went on to say that more than 300,000 beds were needed across the country to accommodate the current student body. By April 2013, DHET (2013) had drafted a policy on student housing that regulates the size, location, amenities, repair, and governance of residences. In September 2015, the DHET (2015) draft became policy. In early October 2015, a leader with the Economic Freedom Fighters, a national political party, tweeted pictures of student residents at the University of Venda. The facilities were in poor condition and the tweet indicated that they were infested with bugs. At the same time, Nelson Mandela Metropolitan University made news for working with a private construction company to expand student housing on campus. Student housing and food continues to be a serious challenge, but both government and university leadership have taken action to ameliorate the situation.

Affordability

If the recent student protests are any indication, affordability is the most pressing issue for students in South Africa. As mentioned in the introduction, the student-led protest movement, called #FeesMustFall, began at the University of Witwatersrand and has since spread across South Africa. Students cite the rising cost of college, the outsourcing of labor, and the poor condition of facilities. Protests escalated when the national government proposed a fee increase of 10% for the 2016 academic year. Some protests shut down universities and became violent, although most were peaceful. These protests have been the largest in the country since the end of apartheid in 1994. After protests at the country's capital, Pretoria, President Jacob Zuma agreed not to increase fees in 2016 and to appoint a committee to consider funding problems. Although the official report has not been released, the committee has acknowledged that the National Student Financial Aid Scheme (NSFAS) is 4.5 billion rand short and the university block grant budget is 2.3 billion rand short.

College leaders have been quick to assert that it is not possible to offer a world-class education without increased funding, particularly with pressure to increase enrollment. The national budget for higher education falls into three big categories: block grants, student funding, and restructuring funds (Wangenge-Ouma, 2010). Block grants are distributed based on teaching and research inputs. Student funding is distributed using the NSFAS that is similar to federal financial aid in the United States. Finally, restructuring dollars are used to assist institutions that are merging or dividing. About 80% of funding is used for block grants, whereas funding for restructuring is disappearing. Researchers have found that although the dollars spent on higher education is increasing, funding per student and as a percentage of gross domestic product has declined since 1995 (Menon, 2015; Wangenge-Ouma, 2010). Increasing tuition and fees is a viable way to balance the decreased per-student funding and continue to grow universities. However, students feel the strain, and government grants and bursaries are not sufficient to cover costs.

From the institutional vantage point, Gyimah-Brempong and Ondiege (2011) noted that the government supplies about 40% of the funding for public colleges and universities. In the years following 1994, national funding for universities of technology declined and fees increased (De Villiers & Steyn, 2009). The reasoning behind the funding shift was to encourage expanded enrollment of Black students at traditional and comprehensive universities; however, recently the need for practical skills in the marketplace has resulted in a policy shift to increase funding for technical universities and decreased funding for comprehensive and traditional universities. Whatever the mix, as the cost of providing an education rises, college leaders are forced to transfer the increases to students or cancel plans for college growth. Both choices will negatively affect the transformation goals of the country.

As mentioned previously, students apply for aid through a process called NSFAS Means Test that uses family income and resources to determine the amount of aid then aid is dispersed by universities. However, students do not receive a guaranteed amount as with the Pell Grant or other need-based program in the United States. Rather, colleges are given a portion of the student funding budget to distribute based on a formula that includes the racial makeup of the college. College financial aid offices then distribute funds to students using the means test as the basis. Colleges also work with private companies to offer bursaries to graduates in high-need areas like engineering and health. Despite these funding opportunities, Letseka and Maile (2008) found that 40% of first-year students drop out because of financial strain. The cost of college and the associated living expenses continues to discourage college enrollment, persistence, and completion.

Accreditation

Qualifications (or degrees types) are linked to accreditation. The National Qualifications Framework (NQF) is a top-down framework of qualification recognition based on outcomes that begins with primary education at NQF 1 and ends with doctoral education at NQF 10 (South African Qualifications Authority [SAQA], 2012). Postsecondary education starts at level NQF 5 (McGrath & Nickola, 2008). In order for an institution to offer qualifications, the minister of education has to assign the institution the authority to do so through the Programme Qualifications Mix (PQM) (Cross, 2015). The NQF is administered based on three subframeworks and three associated accrediting bodies, called Quality Councils, that ensure outcomes are being assessed and met: Council on Higher Education (CHE), Council for Quality Assurance in General and Further Education and Training (UMALUSI), and Quality Council for Trades & Occupations (QCTO). The Quality Councils assess new degrees and programs as well as applications for reaccreditation by schools and universities.

Universities of technology and comprehensive universities can offer degrees from NQF 5 all the way up to NQF 10, as long as they have been approved by the PQM and the student has proven mastery of the outcomes listed by the SAQA. The approval process begins with the number of notional hours (lectures, study time, tutoring, and exams) expected for a student to achieve an outcome. Ten notional hours are equivalent to one credit hour and each qualification level has a minimum number of required credit hours. For example, at NQF 5, students must complete 120 credit hours, which would earn them a certificate. At the bachelor's level, students must earn 480 credits.

Allais (2007) argued that a system like the NQF will not work in its present form. The scholar argued that one cannot build a system of educational qualifications based on outcomes that are detached from a discipline. "The idea that educational quality can be judged against an outcome statement developed out of the context of educational programmes or institutions similarly does not work" (p. 538). Allais reasoned that outcomes cannot be specified to a point at which they are measurable if these outcomes are separated from the field of study.

Machanick (2000) contended that short-term qualifications and trade-focused programs have been oversold by the NQF and the value of education has been misrepresented. Machanick concluded that both the comprehensive and technical universities should focus educational outcomes on marketplace skills.

Transfer

In the United States, students commonly earn a 2-year technical degree or a liberal arts and sciences degree at a community college and transfer to a 4-year institution to complete an academic bachelor's degree. Prior to the NQF, transfer and articulation between racialized institutions was nearly impossible. The governing bodies for the technikons and universities would not consider transfers from vocational colleges and only rarely agreed to articulation arrangements between technical degrees (technikons) and academic degrees (universities) (McGrath & Nickola, 2008).

With the NQF, universities of technology adhere to the same outcomes at NQF 5 as comprehensive and traditional universities (Maserumule, 2005; Raju, 2006). The policy change, as well as the mergers, blurred the lines between institutional types. For example, the University of Witwatersrand, the University of Venda, and Central University of Technology will all have to fulfill the same national standards and requirements for the level of education offered.

In theory, the NQF made it possible for students to transfer or work up the qualifications framework; however, in practice, the quality councils do not articulate levels. Ensor (2004) noted that completing modules according to one's needs and interests might be a good idea in theory, but knowledge in one area cannot build upon knowledge from another. As the NQF is decoupled from a discipline, in theory, one could complete the outcomes from one disciple and switch to another field in which the student has no prior knowledge. This problem made a policy governing the recognition of prior learning necessary. Students earning an NQF 5 certificate can apply for transfer using the recognition of prior learning policy, but it is cumbersome and not seamless (Netswera & Mathabe, 2006; Raju, 2006; SAQA, 2013). The receiving institution's administration determines the admission requirement and the amount of credits they will accept (McGrath & Nickola, 2008).

Because the NQF levels exist separately from the discipline, and comprehensive universities and universities of technology serve a different purpose, a smooth transition, where credits earned at one institution can all articulate to another institution, might be farfetched. Raju (2006) indicated that a new set of guidelines would be required to assist the articulation of different credits. In July 2014, the Department of Higher Education and Training (2014) issued a policy statement intended to respond to the criticism that institutional types were blurred by the NQF and that mission creep was a problem. The policy places the responsibility for articulation and transfer clearly within governmental realms, meaning that institution-based articulation agreements are discouraged.

Future Trends

The recent protests of #RhodesMustFall and #FeesMustFall are an indication that the students at higher educational institutions in South Africa feel that change is needed. These protests have made clear that students would like to see tributes and statues to historic figures who were notorious racists removed. Students believe that access should not be predicated on the ability to pay and that university funds should not make private corporations wealthy through outsourcing.

In addition, the language of instruction is highly continuous. Stellenbosch, a traditional university, has been at the center at the debate. Open Stellenbosch is a student-led movement to remove the evidence of apartheid from campus, including Afrikaans as a language of instruction (Areff, 2015). Afrikaans has long been considered the language of oppression and is primarily spoken by the white minority; however, faculty all over South Africa have developed lectures and curriculum material in Afrikaans. Changing to another language is a challenge for them and a sizable project. In response to protests, management agreed to offer curriculum in languages other than Afrikaans. Most recently, the High Court in Western Cape ordered the campus leaders to follow the campus language policy requiring Afrikaans (Gernetzky, 2016). The protests and debates continue as we write.

Free college will not solve the persistence or preparedness issue. At a 2016 African National Congress (ANC) meeting, South Africa's minister of education stated that the educational system is in crisis after more than a fourth of all students failed their end of the term examination (Nkosi, 2016). These national examinations are given to high-school seniors who are on track to graduate from high school. The 25% of the population who failed mostly come from poorer, rural areas and most of them are Black. These trends make clear the importance of improving secondary education so that students are prepared for college work.

Finally, South Africa is importing workers in science-, engineering-, and technology-related jobs because of a critical shortage of qualified workers in this sector. With an unemployment rate of around 25%, training South Africans to take these positions is an economic imperative. The government has set targets for colleges to increase student enrollment in these fields, and they have funded infrastructure development in these disciplinary areas (Gyimah-Brempong & Ondiege, 2011). Comprehensive universities are well positioned to develop curriculum, programs, and infrastructure to meet these needs much like the ever-flexible American community college.

Conclusion

Numerous countries have used institutional mergers to restructure their higher education systems in attempts to increase access, equity, efficiency, diversity, and quality, as has South Africa (Harman & Harman, 2003; Harman & Meek, 2002). By merging historically White and Black universities, the government attempted to defragment the field of higher education and build financially strong and diverse institutions that are nimble and able to respond to the countries' needs (Gyimah-Brempong & Ondiege, 2011; Menon, 2015). Since the mergers, the higher education landscape in South Africa continues to change quickly, and the national government has shown a willingness to build, adjust, and dismantle policy structures repeatedly. For example, a new bill was introduced in January 2016 that revises the

NQF and gives more authority to SAQA to ensure that colleges are taking steps to meet their transformation goals. This bill reduces institutional autonomy, and gives more authority of the director of higher education. In part, the bill responds to many of the student protest complaints. In this environment, it is grueling for institutions to keep up with the changes, and challenging for researchers to understand whether policies are working. However, no one can dispute their goal of a South Africa that is deracialized and democratic with access to postsecondary education for all.

References

Allais, S. M. (2007). Why the South African NQF Failed: Lessons for countries wanting to introduce national qualifications frameworks. *European Journal of Education, 42*(4), 523–547.

Areff, A. (2015, November 13). English to be main language of instruction at Stellenbosch University. News 24. Retrieved from http://www.news24.com/SouthAfrica/Ne ws/english-to-be-main-language-of-instruction-at-stellenbosch-university-20151113

Collins, K., & Millard, M. (2013). Transforming education in South Africa: Comparative perceptions of a South African social work learning experience. *Educational Review, 65*(1), 70–84.

Cross, M. (2015). State power, transition and new modes of coordination in higher education in South Africa. In S. Schwartzman, R. Pinheiro, & P. Pillay (Eds.), *Higher education in the BRICS countries: Investigating the pact between higher education and society* (pp. 353–376). Dordrecht, Netherlands: Springer.

Council on Higher Education. (2016). *South African higher education reviewed: Two decades of democracy.* Retrieved from http://www.che.ac.za/sites/default/files/ publications/CHE_South%20African%20higher%20education%20reviewed%20-%20 electronic.pdf

Department of Higher Education and Training. (2012). *Report on the Ministerial Committee for the Review of the Provision of Student Housing at South African Universities.* Pretoria, South Africa: Department of Higher Education and Training.

Department of Higher Education and Training. (2013). *Statistics on post-school education and training in South Africa: 2013.* Pretoria, South Africa: Department of Higher Education and Training.

Department of Higher Education and Training. (2014). *Policy framework on differentiation in the South African post-school system.* Pretoria, South Africa: Department of Higher Education and Training.

Department of Higher Education and Training. (2015). *White paper for post-school education and training: Building an expanded, effective and integrated post-school system.* Pretoria, South Africa: Department of Higher Education and Training.

De Villiers, P., & Steyn, G. (2009). Effect of changes in state funding of higher education on education output in South Africa: 1986–2007. *South African Journal of Higher Education, 23*(1), 43–68.

Ensor, P. (2004). Contesting discourses in higher education curriculum restructuring in South Africa. *Higher Education, 48*(3), 339–359.

Gernetzky, K. (2016, March 11). Stellenbosch University ordered to implement "equal language" plan. *Business Day.* Retrieved from http://www.bdlive.co.za/national/educa tion/2016/03/11/stellenbosch-university-ordered-to-implement-equal-language-plan

Gyimah-Brempong, K., & Ondiege, P. (2011). Reforming higher education: Access, equity, and financing in Botswana, Ethiopia, Kenya, South Africa, and Tunisia. *African*

Competitiveness Report. Retrieved from http://www3.weforum.org/tools/afcr2011/pdf/Chap_2_1_Reforming_Higher_Education.pdf

Harman, G., & Harman, K. (2003). Institutional mergers in higher education: Lessons from international experience. *Tertiary Education and Management, 9*(1), 29–44.

Harman, K., & Meek, V. L. (2002). Introduction to special issues: "Merger revisited: international perspectives on mergers in higher education." *Higher Education, 44*(1), 1–4.

Higher Education Management Information System. (2012). *Open Data 2000–2012.* Retrieved from https://dl.dropboxusercontent.com/u/9480369/DATA%20SA%20HE%20 2012%20Data%20Updated%20March%202014.zip

Letseka, M., & Maile, S. (2008). *High university drop-out rates: A threat to South Africa's future* (HSRC Research Outputs 5729). Pretoria, South Africa: Human Sciences Research Council. Retrieved from http://www.hsrc.ac.za/en/research-data/view/4274

Machanick, P. (2000). On the value of qualifications: Why go to university or technikon? Retrieved from http://citeseerx.ist.psu.edu/viewdoc/download?doi= 10.1.1.38.9389&rep=rep1&type=pdf

Maserumule, M. H. (2005). Designating technikons universities of technology in South Africa: Implications for public management education. *African Journal of Public Administration and Management, 16*(1), 14–27.

McGrath, P. J., & Nickola, L. (2008). *A new education framework and the impact on vocational qualifications offered by South African comprehensive universities and universities of technology.* Retrieved from http://uir.unisa.ac.za/bitstream/handle/ 10500/2930/nikola.pdf

Menon, K. (2015). Supply and demand in South Africa. In S. Schwartzman, R. Pinheiro, & P. Pillay (Eds.), *Higher education in the BRICS countries: Investigating the pact between higher education and society* (pp. 171–190). Dordrecht, Netherlands: Springer.

Ministry of Education. (2001). *National plan for higher education.* Retrieved from http://chet.org.za/manual/media/files/chet_hernana_docs/South%20Africa/National/ National%20Plan%20for%20HE%20SA.pdf

Netswera, F. G., & Mathabe, N. (2006). A pervasive apartheid? An analysis of changing higher education in South Africa and its relationship with the state. *Journal of Educational Administration and History, 38*(1), 29–40. doi:10.1080/00220620600552425

Nkosi, M. (2016, January 29). Is South Africa's education system really "in crisis"? *BBC News.* Retrieved from http://www.bbc.com/news/world-africa-35427853

Raju, J. (2006). The historical evolution of university and technikon education and training in South Africa and its implications for articulations between the two types of higher educational institutions with particular references to LIS education and training. Retrieved from http://ir.dut.ac.za/bitstream/handle/10321/404/Raju_2006.pdf

Soudien, C. (2010). The reconstitution of privilege: Integration in former white schools in South Africa. *Journal of Social Issues, 66*(2), 352–366.

South African Qualifications Authority. (2012). *Level descriptors for the South African National Qualifications Framework.* Waterkloof, South Africa: South African Qualifications Authority.

South African Qualifications Authority. (2013). *National policy for the implementation of the recognition of prior learning.* Waterkloof, South Africa: South African Qualifications Authority.

U.S. Department of Education. (2012). Enrollment trends by age. *Digest of Education Statistics,* Table 7. Retrieved from https://nces.ed.gov/programs/coe/pdf/ Indicator_CEA/COE_CEA_2013_01.pdf

Wangenge-Ouma, G. (2010). Funding and the attainment of transformation goals in South Africa's higher education. *Oxford Review of Education, 36*(4), 481–497.

KRISTIN BAILEY WILSON in an associate professor in the Department of Educational Administration, Leadership and Research at Western Kentucky University. Her research concerns with marginalized populations attending community college. She was recently awarded a Fulbright to South Africa.

WOUTER VAN ALEBEEK is a doctoral student in educational leadership (This is the proper name of the program) at Western Kentucky University. He is interested in research on international students and schools and has spent considerable time in South Africa.

NEW DIRECTIONS FOR COMMUNITY COLLEGES • DOI: 10.1002/cc

8

This chapter compares the role of institutional and national completion agendas at community colleges and global counterparts around the world.

Comparing Completion Agendas at Community Colleges and Global Counterparts

Rosalind Latiner Raby, Janice Nahra Friedel, Edward J. Valeau

Currently, no other institutional type is found in as many countries as the community college and its global counterpart. These institutions have been extensively studied in a comparative mode since the 1960s (Eddy, 2014; Raby & Tarrow, 1996; Wiseman, Chase-Mayoral, Janis, & Sachdev, 2012); it is known that they vary substantially in their organizational structure, their mission, and even their curriculum. The common thread, however, is that these institutions offer a more advanced curriculum than secondary schools and serve as a local and often lower cost pathway that gives options for university overflow for adult learners, displaced workers, lifelong learners, workforce learners, developmental learners, and nontraditional learners (Raby & Valeau, 2009, p. 1). These institutions are known by several names including colleges of further education, community colleges, polytechnic, technical colleges, and TAFE (technical and further education).

This chapter begins with a discussion on the role of completion agendas at community colleges and global counterparts. Unlike the United States, where the community college completion agenda has been a focus of discussion and debate for a decade, similar discourse is less known among global counterparts. We define completion as a prescribed set of requirements that are finished by the student during a noted period of time for one or more of the following: (a) short-term certificates, diplomas, or industry skill credentials; (b) multiyear coursework leading to an associate degree and graduation; and (c) multiyear course work leading to the ability to transfer to a university. To arrive at our definition, we surveyed 41 administrators from 25 community colleges and global counterparts to see how they define completion and how they depict the ways in which this agenda is being implemented.

New Directions for Community Colleges, no. 177, Spring 2017 © 2017 Wiley Periodicals, Inc.
Published online in Wiley Online Library (wileyonlinelibrary.com) • DOI: 10.1002/cc.20244

Completion: A Comparative Overview

The completion agenda is a by-product of a changing era that links community college and global counterpart completion to criteria essential for workforce entry (Organisation for Economic Co-operation and Development [OECD], 2014). Success is seen as a result of programs and services that improve educational outcomes, workforce preparedness, and close achievement gaps for historically underrepresented students by increasing the change that students finish their educational programs. Comparative research explores why completion may not occur, elements leading to completion success, and emerging policies.

Why Completion May Not Occur.   Although the literature acknowledges that student learning styles can contribute to a lack of success, studies also focus on college policies and other sorting mechanisms that truncate success. Clark (1960) refers to these as a "cooling out" process, in which students are tracked into programs and classes depending on their social class. In this context, individual aspirations are curtailed, which has a negative impact on achievement and completion. Specific examples are found in completion literature about institutional practices at U.S. community colleges (Calcagno, Crosta, Bailey, & Jenkins, 2007; Center for Community College Student Engagement, 2013), at British colleges of further education (Harbour & Ozan, 2007), and at Mexican universidades tecnologicas (Gregorutti, 2012). Although the overall international completion rates for those attending community colleges and global counterparts are low, some stability has been seen over the past few years (OECD, 2014).

Elements Leading to Completion Success.   Despite documented barriers, comparative research shows how community college and global counterpart students can take educational paths that result in unique examples of completion. For some, success is based on course-specific learning (UNESCO, 2015) as students may not be enrolled in a specific multi-course program. Herault, Zakirova, and Buddelmeyer (2012) show that in Australia, participation in even some tertiary education at a TAFE institution brings higher wage earning. In addition, elements leading to success can stem from specific programmatic changes, such as student-focused reforms in Senegal (Gueye & Sene, 2009), quality assurance programs in Qatar (Spangler & Tyler, 2011), and entrepreneurial education programs in Canada (Nixon, 2011). Literature about Vietnamese community colleges (World Bank, 2008), Indian global counterparts (Kingdon, 2007), and women at Japanese junior colleges (Anazi & Paik, 2012), shows that those who complete their programs have increased job prospects. Shumaker (2013) notes that in 2012, 82% of graduates of Tunisian higher institutes of technological studies found jobs within 6 months of graduation (Shumaker, 2013). Evidence of success remains a primary reason students choose to attend community colleges and global counterparts. It is important to note that these studies do not indicate whether jobs attained are commensurate with level of study achieved (Raby & Valeau, 2009).

Emerging Policies.   A growing number of studies focus on policies intended to improve completion at community colleges and their global counterparts. Many of these publications define the role of governmental policies in influencing institutional actions to increase completion rates. Such publications highlight government policies that define and/or monitor student completion policies in Turkey (World Bank, 2007), in England (Longden, 2012–2013), in Ireland (Kerr, 2006), and in New Zealand (Scott, 2009). These policies share similarity in their focus to get students to finish their programs. Completion is also noted in institutional policies at British Columbia community colleges (Andres, 2009) and in policies that target how to foster student success at Canadian community colleges for Aboriginal students (King, 2008).

Methodology

This is the first comparative examination of the completion agenda in a range of community colleges and global counterparts. Purposeful sampling was based on an open call to members of eight international electronic mailing lists to gather the opinions of those who are actively involved in cross-national partnerships through international development projects and student mobility projects and those who are involved in comparative studies on community colleges and global counterparts. All respondents defined their institutions as fitting into the definition of a community college and global counterpart (Raby & Valeau, 2009).

We used a web-based survey with open-ended style that was first administered in winter 2012 to 16 respondents for a pilot survey. Based on responses, questions were edited for clarity and readministered to the same individuals and to new contacts in spring 2013 for a total of 41 respondents from 25 countries.

Data were coded to quantify who responded to the survey in terms of institutional position and the extent of knowledge of existing completion policies. Data were then coded for institutional profile, accreditation agency, baseline completion data, and type of student cohorts being tracked. Questions were designed to allow respondents to give personal accounts of how (a) completion agenda affected their professional duties, (b) policies affected student success, (c) government financial incentives affected results, and (d) challenges affected the completion agenda. Respondents provided three national completion policy weblinks, six college websites, and one baseline data report in English that were then reviewed to assess overall content.

This sample represents the perspectives of specific individuals and does not seek to generalize or to make supporting claims. Yet, it does uncover

NEW DIRECTIONS FOR COMMUNITY COLLEGES • DOI: 10.1002/cc

knowledge of similarities and differences held by practitioners in the community college and global counterpart sector.

Results

Survey responses provided information on descriptive statistics of the structure of community college and global counterparts, overview of issues related to completion, and identified challenges in the field.

Descriptive Statistics. Survey respondents confirm that structural and curricula designs vary among community colleges and global counterparts (Raby & Valeau, 2009). A majority (62.5%) of the responding institutions offered 1- to 3-year certificates and associate degrees, of which 22.2% had options for bachelor's and master's degrees and 6% offered teacher training certificates. The remaining 37.5% offered certificates resulting from less than a year of study, of which 4% offered short-term student mobility transcripts of completion. Of all responding institutions, 76% offered a multifocus curriculum (combination of academic and vocational-technical studies) and only seven institutions allowed transfer to a 4-year university.

Positions held by the respondents were as follows: 82.8% coordinators or directors and 6% college presidents. A total of 52.3% worked at a global counterpart in Australia, China, Denmark, Finland, Holland, Hungary, India, Jamaica, Latvia, Lithuania, New Zealand, Norway, Pakistan, Singapore, Sweden, Taiwan, Tobago, and United Kingdom, and 36.5% worked at a U.S. community college involved in a partnership with global counterparts in Bolivia, Brazil, Canada, China, Costa Rica, Korea, Mexico, and Vietnam. The remaining 11.2% of respondents were university faculty who conducted research at community college global counterparts in China, Ethiopia, Indonesia, Israel, Mexico, Uganda, and Zambia.

Who Is Responsible for Overseeing Policies. Similar to Raby and Valeau (2009) who define various organizational patterns in which community college and global counterparts are managed, survey respondents confirmed a range of accreditation bodies, of which 52.8% named the ministry of education, 19.6% named the ministry of higher education, 13.1% named the ministry of economy, 11.3% named the ministry of labor and employment, and 3.2% named the ministry for vocational education. In addition, 16.7 % also said that a secondary accreditation body included a local university system. The mission of each accreditation body is reflected in the range of completion agenda patterns noted by survey respondents.

Overview of Issues Related to Completion. A range of data emerged from survey respondents on national completion agendas and about half provided details of institutional metrics, such as when they were initiated, how they are measured, how students are tracked, and national financial rewards for completion.

National Policies and Goals. About half of respondents said that they did not know of existing completion policies or skipped these questions entirely. Even among the U.S. respondents, none noted that policies existed and one stated that "the variety of colleges in the United States and the focus on state-level policies do not support any national policies." A respondent from Mexico said that the Subsecretaria de Educacion Superior (2013) policy does not list completion as a priority. A respondent from Israel referred to a report by the Israeli State Comptroller (2008) that "pointed out very low completion rates (less than 50%) and called for reform in the budget/finance of colleges to encourage them to improve completion rates." This respondent, however, noted that the report has not resulted in a national policy.

The remaining respondents referred to existing national policies. One respondent reported the "Danish Ministry of Higher Education and Science goals of having 95% pass a youth education certificate, which would result in 60% of each cohort of youth then completing the level of higher education" and said that the rate is currently at 45–48%. One respondent noted a goal is to "half the proportion of Australians aged 20–64 without qualifications at Certificate III and above, and to double the number of higher qualification completions (diploma and advanced diploma) over the next 10 years." Another respondent from Australia noted that a "national policy is administered by the Department of Education and Training (2013), Australian Tertiary Education Quality (2013) and Standards Agency and Australian Skills Quality Authority (2013) and that each of these have their own completion agenda criteria, and yet they complement one another nicely." Yet another respondent from Australia elaborated on an "early help system that is used before the student is in major trouble with his/her studies, and that offers special workshops for the students and that even provides assistance for those about to and who have already dropped out." A respondent from China noted that a national goal in China, "monitored by the Ministry of Education, (2012) sets goals and measures the completion rates of HEI students in general, and of students who attend Vocational Colleges, in particular." Finally, several respondents revealed that national completion policies exist in Hungary, Sweden, and India but did not provide links to or description of these policies.

Several participants noted institutionally specific programs that aim to increase the number of those who finish specific educational programs. A respondent from Tobago Community College detailed an institutional policy in which "students must finish 75 credit hours, must take three courses in English composition and vocabulary, one semester in World History, one semester course in citizenship, and one course in multiethnic studies." A respondent from Roskilde Business College in Denmark noted different completion policies for the 2-year diploma programs, the academy profession degree programs, and the bachelor's degree programs. Finally, one respondent shared a personal opinion that "students [in Singapore at the Institute of Technical Education] pay hefty sums so I think family pressure for completion is a significantly bigger factor than any college policy."

How Students Are Followed. Few details were given on how colleges track student process. One respondent from a college in China said that the college "tracks high school students who take a Gap Program at the college as well as those who complete the two-year academic program." A respondent from Tobago Community College said that the college "tracks all students who are in an associate degree program and can identify those who finished their degree and those who have not finished their coursework. Such assessment is done through examination at the completion of each term." A respondent from Box Hill College in Australia said that "all minors (under 18) are tracked and there is a measurement in terms of identifying the percentage of those who completed their studies in 3 years." It is evident that more research needs to be done in this area.

Financial Rewards for Completion. Questions relating to financial incentives to push for completion were answered in the negative by 75% of respondents. A common viewpoint is explained by one respondent that in many countries "financial aid in the form of grants or scholarships to economically poor students is nonexistent." A few respondents did, however, note a connection of such aid to student persistence. One example where financial incentives exist is in Jamaica where the respondent said that "special funds are given to the colleges for supporting dropouts and those in danger of dropout. These grants have been given out by the ministry lately." The use of financial incentives was given as an example by all the respondents from Australia, one of whom said "there is an additional 'taximeter' connected to completion." The two respondents from Lithuania and from Latvia both noted that the national government provides financial support to well-performing students.

Discussion on Identified Challenges in the Field. Survey respondents indicated that there are three challenges to enacting a viable completion agenda. First, who defines quality assurance and accreditation presents unique challenges because in many countries, multiple agencies are responsible in defining success. Moreover, the impetus for reform varies from a national level (as in Indonesia) to local university policies (as in Israel) or to institutional policies (as in Denmark). The conflict between agencies was noted by several respondents as a key challenge. Respondents from China, Ethiopia, and India echoed the respondent from Tobago who noted that "who defines quality assurances is then responsible for redefining faculty qualifications which are at the foundation for student success."

Second, financial challenges from the changing global economy affect institutional abilities to implement a completion agenda. One respondent from India noted that "politicization determines whether financial assistance is given to colleges and that assistance determines the level to which policies can be fully implemented." A respondent from Denmark noted that the "increase of the world economic crisis will have resulting changes in the political environment which will influence the higher education community." Finally, almost all of the respondents indicated that student personal finance is a critical issue in completion.

Finally, there is a perceived challenge that links success to varying degrees of individual student motivation. The Tobago respondent noted a challenge "is how to sensitize students to make them accept their responsibility as future leaders of Tobago and the global society." An Australian respondent noted that a challenge "lies within the 5–15 percent of students that may not be fully prepared for higher educational programmes and the challenges hereby." Another respondent from Australia noted that "many young people are persuaded and rewarded for entering higher education programmes, meaning that not all of them have intrinsic motivation to complete." The need to increase the motivation of students was also mentioned as a challenge by a China respondent in terms of "increasing the student overall awareness."

Conclusion

The completion agenda at community colleges and global counterparts is not well understood, documented, or discussed in the literature. This absence forms the basis of this chapter's intent to expand our knowledge of the completion agenda. In so doing, this chapter details cross-national similarities in which prescribed requirements exist to guide students to ultimately obtain certificates, diplomas, or skill credentials. Through a purposive sampling based on an open call to members of eight international electronic mailing lists, the opinions of lower level administrators illustrate the extent to which completion policies exist at a variety of institutions and how they are perceived to affect daily operations.

Summary results provide information on two structural elements of community colleges and global counterparts. First is the range of curricula emphasis and credential/degree focus. The second is the responsibility for overseeing policies among the participants that range from the ministry of education to the ministry of labor and employment. The similarities also extend to the level of authority between administrators that affect decision making and sustained efforts toward a completion agenda. The final similarity is that many survey participants had limited information on national policies and in particular, how those policies are enacted at their institutions.

The importance of this study lies in its effort to establish a comparative focus on community colleges and global counterparts. It provides foundational information on perceptions of the application of policy and on the discussion of completion in an international context. Although classification of these institutions is evolving and is diverse, noted commonalities of mission to serve local communities and nontraditional students prominently exist. This chapter argues that these institutions also now share and are expanding a focus on building student completion policies.

NEW DIRECTIONS FOR COMMUNITY COLLEGES • DOI: 10.1002/cc

As this occurs, a variety of circumstances contribute to student completion policies not being uniform across institutions. Some in this sector have deep historical roots whereas others are newly developed. Even more, some are part of a defined national higher educational system that must adhere to national policies, whereas others are more independently operated. Some have extensive financial support and others are rooted in impoverished conditions. As such, differences in definitions of success as well as in the effectiveness of institutional policies are to be expected. However, it is encouraging to note that at the 25 institutions studied, there is a discussion emerging on the importance of student completion and what institutional policies need to occur to facilitate that completion.

As the literature evolves around the topic and leaders seek to establish new policies and programs around the completion agenda efforts to learn more, we offer some suggestions for future comparative studies:

1. Examination, in more detail, of how a completion agenda is perceived differently across state and national governmental agencies via policy development and defined programs and activities.
2. Examination of implementation of matrices for national comparisons of like institutions. Thus, it is vitally important to examine the implications of these policies on persistence and success of future generations of students.
3. Identification of specific pathways in terms of using institutional goals and/or state or national policy as it relates to community college global counterparts.
4. Identification of how educational policies are being enacted, monitored, and then used toward achieving specific goals related to completion in global community counterparts.

We conclude that the completion agenda has much to offer when examined in a comparative focus and hope that this study helps to further the dialog.

References

Andres, L. (2009). *The dynamics of post-secondary participation and completion: A fifteen year portrayal of BC young adults.* Vancouver, BC: British Columbia Council on Admissions and Transfer. (ED508700)

Anazi, S., & Paik, C. M. (2012). Factors influencing Japanese women to choose two-year colleges in Japan. *Community College Journal of Research and Practice, 36*(8), 614–625.

Australian Tertiary Education Quality and Standards Agency. (2013). Homepage. Retrieved from http://www.teqsa.gov.au/

Calcagno, J. C., Crosta, P., Bailey, T., & Jenkins, D. (2007). Stepping stones to a degree: The impact of enrollment pathways and milestones on older community college students. *Research in Higher Education, 48*(4), 775–801.

Center for Community College Student Engagement. (2013). *A matter of degrees: Engaging practices, engaging students (high-impact practices for community college student engagement)*. Austin, TX: University of Texas at Austin, Community College Leadership Program.

Chinese Ministry of Education. (2012). Business. Retrieved from http://www.moe.edu.cn/publicfiles/business/htmlfiles/moe/s7566/index.html2

Clark, B. (1960). The cooling-out function in higher education. *American Journal of Sociology, 65*(6), 569–576.

Department of Education and Training. (2013). Homepage. Retrieved from http://www.education.vic.gov.au/Pages/default.aspx

Eddy, P. L. (2014). Special issue: Community colleges and their internationalization efforts. *Community College Journal of Research and Practice, 38*(8). doi: 10.1080/10668926.2014.897077

Gregorutti, G. (2012). The Mexican idea of two-year university degrees: A model of opportunities and challenges. In A. W. Wiseman, A. Chase-Mayoral, T. Janis, & A. Sachdev (Eds.), *Community colleges worldwide: Investigating the global phenomenon* (pp. 49–71). Bingley, UK: Emerald Publishing.

Gueye, B., & Sene, I. (2009). A critical approach to the community college model in the global order: The *College Universitaire Régional* of Bambey (Senegal) as a case study. In R. L. Raby & E. Valeau (Eds.), *Community college models: Globalization and higher education reform* (pp. 235–251). Dordrecht, The Netherlands: Springer.

Harbour, C. P., & Ozan, J. (2007). Advancing an equity agenda at the community college in an age of privatization, performance accountability, and marketization. *Equity & Excellence in Education, 40*(3), 197–207.

Herault, N., Zakirova, R., & Buddelmeyer, H. (2012). *The effect of VET completion on the wages of young people*. Adelaide, South Australia: National Centre for Vocational Education Research.

Israeli State Comptroller. (2008). Activities of the institute for training in technology and science (ITTS) [Hebrew]. *Annual Report, 59*(2). Jerusalem: Author.

Kerr, M. (2006). Funding systems and their effects on higher education systems: Country study—Ireland. Paris, France: Organisation for Economic Co-operation and Development. Retrieved from http://www.oecd.org/education/skills-beyond-school/38308018.pdf

King, T. (2008). Fostering Aboriginal leadership: Increasing enrollment and completion rates in Canadian post-secondary institutions. *College Quarterly, 11*(1), 1–16.

Kingdon, G. G. (2007). *The progress of school in India*. Oxford, UK: Global Poverty Research Group, Department of Economics, University of Oxford.

Longden, B. (2012–2013). Bearing down on student non-completion: Implications and consequences for English higher education. *Journal of College Student Retention: Research, Theory & Practice, 14*(1), 117–147.

Nixon, G. (2011). Revenue generation through training a global energy workforce. In S. Sutin, D. Derrico, E. Valeau, & R. L. Raby (Eds.), *Increasing effectiveness of the community college financial model: A global perspective for the global economy* (pp. 225–239). New York, NY: Palgrave Macmillan.

Organisation for Economic Co-operation and Development. (2014). *Education at a glance 2014. OCED indicators*. Paris, France: Author. http://dx.doi.org/10.1787/eng-2014-en

Raby, R. L., & Tarrow, N. (Eds.). (1996). *Dimensions of the community college: International and inter/multicultural perspectives. Garland Studies in Higher Education: Vol. 6. Garland Reference Library of Social Science: Vol. 1075*. New York, NY: Garland.

Raby, R. L., & Valeau, E. (2009). *Community college models: Globalization and higher education reform*. Dordrecht, The Netherlands: Springer.

Scott, D. J. (2009). A closer look at completion in higher education in New Zealand. *Journal of Higher Education Policy & Management, 31*(2), 101–108.

Shumaker, J. W. (2013). U.S. community colleges and a response to the Arab Spring. In T. Treat & L. S. Hagedorn (Eds.), *New Directions for Community Colleges: No. 161. Community college in a global context* (pp. 114–126). San Francisco: Jossey-Bass. doi: 10.1002/cc.

Spangler, M. S., & Tyler, A., Jr. (2011). A Houston-Doha partnership: Leveraging local assets to create a global enterprise. *International Educator, 20*(4), 54–57.

Standards Agency and Australian Skills Quality Authority. (2013). Homepage. Retrieved from http://www.asqa.gov.au/

Subsecretaria de Educacion Superior. (2013). Homepage [Spanish]. Retrieved from http://www.ses.sep.gob.mx/. UNESCO. (2015). *Education for All global monitoring report 2014.* Retrieved from http://www.unesco.org/new/en/education/themes/leading-the-international-agenda/efareport/

Wiseman, A. W., Chase-Mayoral, A., Janis, T., & Sachdev, A. (2012). Community colleges: Where are they (not?). In A. W. Wiseman, A. Chase-Mayoral, T. Janis, & A. Sachdev (Eds.), *Community colleges worldwide: Investigating the global phenomenon* (pp. 3–19). Bingley, UK: Emerald Publishing.

World Bank. (2007). *Turkey: Higher education policy study.* Washington DC: World Bank. Retrieved from http://documents.worldbank.org/curated/en/2007/06/8730072/turkey-higher-education-policy-study

World Bank. (2008). *Vietnam—Higher education and skills for growth.* Washington, DC: World Bank. Retrieved from http://documents.worldbank.org/curated/en/2008/06/10988339/vietnam-higher-education-skills-growth

ROSALIND LATINER RABY, PhD, *is a senior lecturer at California State University, Northridge in the Educational Leadership and Policy Studies Department of the College of Education and is the director of California Colleges for International Education, a nonprofit consortium with 88 California community college members.*

JANICE NAHRA FRIEDEL, PhD, *is an associate professor at the School of Education, College of Human Services at Iowa State University of Science and Technology.*

EDWARD J. VALEAU, EdD, *is superintendent president emeritus of Hartnell Community College (California) where he served for 12 years. He is also president emeritus of California Colleges for International Education and is the founder and senior partner of the ELS Group, a national chief executive search firm located in Northern California.*

9

This chapter describes the expansion of postsecondary or tertiary education throughout the world, the motivations for the expansion, and the commonalities and differences in the systems.

Global Postsecondary Education

George R. Boggs, Paul A. Elsner, Judith T. Irwin

Across the globe, countries are expanding and strengthening postsecondary education systems. In the increasingly global society and economy, education and training beyond customary compulsory primary and secondary education are now seen as essential to a nation's competitiveness and the standard of living of its people. The need to open the doors of higher or further education beyond the relatively limited enrollments in elite and selective universities has spawned a movement to develop or expand institutions that are generally less expensive, more accessible, more flexible, and tied more closely to business and industry. The authors of this chapter have recently worked with more than 50 other authors to profile the postsecondary or tertiary education systems in 35 countries (Elsner, Boggs, & Irwin, 2015). The common thread across the countries studied is a realization of the necessity to prepare their people for a changing, increasingly complex, technologically driven, and interdependent global economy.

Competing in a High-Skilled Global Economy

One of the most significant effects of the global economy was highlighted by the publication, *Tough Choices or Tough Times: The Report of the New Commission on the Skills for the American Workforce* (National Center on Education and the Economy, 2008). The report noted that a worldwide market was developing in which work requiring only low-skill labor would go to those countries where its price was the lowest. If the leadership of a country decides, perhaps by default, to compete in a low-skill environment, the report indicates that it could look forward to an economy built upon low wages and long working hours. Alternatively, policymakers could focus less on low-skill work and set goals to compete in a worldwide market of high-value-added products and services. A high-skill economy, the report authors argue, requires a country to adopt internationally benchmarked

NEW DIRECTIONS FOR COMMUNITY COLLEGES, no. 177, Spring 2017 © 2017 Wiley Periodicals, Inc.
Published online in Wiley Online Library (wileyonlinelibrary.com) • DOI: 10.1002/cc.20245

standards for educating its students and its workers. Informed international leaders have come to realize that countries with highly skilled workforces are the only ones that can successfully compete in the global market. Vocational education in most countries appears to be transformed from older industrial age skills to new higher end competencies in language, math, physics, and chemistry. Innovation-centered occupations, valued code writers, programmers, cybersecurity specialists, digital media design, film production, and imaging technologies in health-related fields represent some of the most rapidly growing high-skilled occupations.

Tom Friedman (2007) made this same point about the global economy characterizing the world as flat. He made the point that businesses and countries can now outsource virtually every job to any place, and work will get done where it can be done most efficiently and effectively. Technology now allows us to view live images of events taking place virtually anywhere in the world—24 hours a day and 7 days a week. We can communicate with people in remote parts of the world, listen to music that suits our desire, or read documents without physically holding them. Text, voice, and images can be transferred with a click on a cell phone or a computer. Jobs that once needed to be done in local communities can now be done anywhere on earth that is connected by technology and inexpensive modes of transport. Moreover, search engines have distributed information more equitably than ever before. Centers of information and expertise that were once controlled by certain nation states or economic powers have become so decentralized that the economies of countries throughout the world have become much more self-organized and less controlled by more developed countries.

Advancing Technology Generates Successful Outcomes

Another significant trend, highlighted in an article in *USA Today* (Webster, 2014), is the displacement of low-skilled workers by advances in technology. Webster's article quotes Carl Benedict Frey, one of the authors of a 2013 University of Oxford study on the future of employment, as saying that 70% of low-skilled jobs may be replaced by robots or other technology in 10 to 20 years. She quotes Henrik Christensen, director of the Institute for Robotics and Intelligent Machines at Georgia Institute of Technology, as saying, " If you are unskilled labor today, you'd better start thinking about getting an education."

Developing a Global Workforce Through Education and Training

The severe global economic recession that began in 2007 provided hard evidence of the importance of education and training. On average across Organisation for Economic Development and Co-operation and Development (OECD) countries, 4.8% of individuals with a tertiary (postsecondary) degree were unemployed in 2011, compared to 12.6% of those lacking a secondary education. Between 2008 and 2011, the unemployment gap between those with low levels of education and those with high levels of education widened: across all age groups, the unemployment rate for less educated individuals increased by almost 3.8 percentage points, whereas it increased by only 1.5 percentage points for highly educated individuals. Without the foundational skills provided by a minimum level of education, people find themselves particularly vulnerable in an insecure labor market. The effect of educational attainment on employment during the economic downturn was even more pronounced for younger people. Across OECD countries, an average of 18.1% of 25- to 34-year-olds without secondary education were unemployed in 2011, compared with 6.8% of those with a tertiary qualification (OECD, 2013).

Just as in the United States, Denmark reported recent across-the-board increases in participation in education and training among young people. These increases can be attributed both to the poor employment prospects during the recent financial recession and to a number of government policies specifically aimed at encouraging young people to enter post-compulsory education at an earlier age. The government in Denmark is currently planning to introduce further measures so that youth who are 25 years or less cannot receive social assistance but instead need to be either in education or working.

Of course, acquisition of skills is not by itself sufficient to lead to increased youth employment. Concerned governments must implement the right economic policies in noneducation sectors to address issues of corruption, quality assurance, and institutional support and capacity in order to encourage manufacturing and other productive industries to stimulate the demand for employable skills.

Officials in less developed countries worry about higher performance standards invoked by Western European countries, such as the United Kingdom, the Netherlands, France, and Germany, all of which have global economies (Elsner, 2015). In the United States, there is concern that some colleges in the for-profit sector are not preparing students adequately for careers that pay enough to permit the students to repay government loans (Mellow, 2014).

Incorporating New Training Models.   Developments in the countries profiled by the authors (Elsner et al., 2015) revealed an understanding that economic cycles, free market capitalism, digital access to markets, Internet-based commerce, and advances in technology call for new training models. Increasing education and skill levels require an emphasis on the types of open and accessible institutions that are most efficient and productive. These institutions go by different names: community colleges, technical colleges, technical universities, polytechnics, further education (FE) institutions, technical and further education (TAFE) institutions, institutes of technology, colleges of technology, and junior colleges. Their evolution has been shaped by the societal needs that have emerged in various regions, political and economic pressures, and the visions of leaders.

The institutions vary as to whether they are public, private, or private for profit. The missions vary as to the level of degrees or qualifications they can award and their focus on vocational-technical education or academic liberal arts. In some countries, they are considered part of the higher education system; in others, there is a marked separation between higher education and further education. In some places, they are part of university systems; in others, they are stand-alone institutions. In some countries, students can transfer credits that they earn in these institutions to other institutions, including universities, to work toward more advanced credentials or degrees; in others, they cannot. In some countries, the institutions are governed centrally; in others, governance systems are localized. Some focus more on younger students; others serve adults and their need for lifelong learning.

Connecting the Dots. What, then, defines this sector? Common elements include, for the most part, open access, a nonelitist orientation, a focus on the success of students in their learning, responsiveness to the educational needs of local communities and their industries, and a willingness to be creative and to avoid bureaucratic processes. In most countries, the institutions lack the prestige of the elite universities even though the well-being of a country and its people usually depend more upon the educational level of the majority rather than a small minority. In the United States, almost half of all students in higher education are enrolled in community colleges, and some of community college alumni have received Nobel prizes or been recognized in other notable ways. Community colleges in the United States educate most of the nation's nurses, fire fighters, police officers, mechanics, and technicians.

Growing Awareness of the U.S. Community College Concept

Recently, there has been an increasing international interest in the American community college model. In July 2009, Dr. Jill Biden, wife of the U.S. vice president and herself a community college faculty member, presented a keynote address at the United Nations Educational, Scientific, and Cultural Organization (UNESCO) World Conference on Higher Education in Paris, encouraging the leaders of developing countries to consider the community college model (Biden, 2009). Community colleges based on the American model have now been established in Saudi Arabia, Qatar, Vietnam, Thailand, and the Republic of Georgia. Representatives from the United Kingdom, Australia, New Zealand, and China have sent delegations to the United States to study community colleges. Representatives from U.S. community colleges have been invited to Jordan, the United Arab Emirates, India, South Africa, and Ukraine to explain the American model and how it might be adapted to fit the cultures of other countries. The

NEW DIRECTIONS FOR COMMUNITY COLLEGES • DOI: 10.1002/cc

American Association of Community Colleges has signed cooperative agreements with postsecondary education systems in Canada, the United Kingdom, Australia, Germany, Denmark, and the Netherlands, and it is a member of the World Federation of Colleges and Polytechnics, an organization dedicated to the global improvement of workforce education and lifelong learning. These agreements and partnerships enable the sharing of promising practices and build bridges of understanding and cooperation.

Even though there is increased interest in the American community college model, the tertiary education models that have developed in other countries can also inform policymakers who want to develop or improve this level of education and training in their own countries. Policymakers need to develop a tertiary education system that fits the culture and needs of their countries, and an examination of the characteristics of different models of postsecondary education is an important first step. Whereas most countries assert clear and focused national priorities for workforce and technical education and training through a central ministry of education, the United States does not. Individual states and sometimes individual colleges set the goals and priorities for education in the United States, rendering the programs more responsive to local education and training needs but also resulting in a lack of consistent accountability measures and a reduced focus on national priorities. Because of the dispersed governance of postsecondary education in the United States, the institutions are slower to change to meet national priorities. The federal government's role in quality assurance is to monitor and approve the agencies that accredit the institutions and to issue regulations that are subject to negotiations and legal action.

Entrepreneurship Education.   Programs in entrepreneurship education have become prevalent in community colleges in the United States, with hundreds of colleges providing education and support for entrepreneurs. The programs range from traditional classroom courses, both credit and noncredit, to support structures such as student business incubators, micro loans and venture capital funding to help would-be entrepreneurs start businesses, and mentorship programs that match students with local entrepreneurial role models. Some community colleges are themselves serving as role models for the entrepreneurial community by undertaking entrepreneurial ventures such as opening a boutique hotel, building a major regional tourist attraction, and operating a publishing arm.

Distinguishing Variances Between the Systems.   In contrast to the American community college model, the British further education institutions are centrally controlled. They undergo periodic inspections from the central government, and institutions can be closed if they do not meet quality and performance goals established by the national funding authorities. The central ministries in China exert full control over certain constitutionally formed universities although they encourage direction but not complete control by local authorities over provincial and local institutions.

NEW DIRECTIONS FOR COMMUNITY COLLEGES • DOI: 10.1002/cc

The strengths of the American model are its accessibility to all who desire education and training; its responsiveness to local community needs and the needs of local industry for skilled labor; and an entrepreneurial spirit that enables the community colleges to build partnerships with other institutions, businesses, and government. One of the most significant advantages of the American model is that it developed as a component of higher education as opposed to a separate further education sector, enabling students to transfer to other educational institutions to build on their education and attain more advanced credentials and degrees. However, the transfer function is not perfect, and students sometimes lose credits for courses they have taken at the community college, and stubborn achievement gaps persist for racial minorities and students from low-income families. A growing number of states are authorizing community colleges to offer bachelor's degrees in addition to certificates and associate degrees, most often in applied or technical subjects.

Incorporating the Apprenticeship Model. There is a growing interest in the United States in the European apprenticeship model. A recent study in Denmark showed that after 12 months following completion, graduates from the school-based apprentice system have as good employment prospects as those who have followed traditional apprentice programs. Similar to college-based internships in the United States, the school apprentice system in Denmark entails work placements in which many students end up finishing their vocational training program from an enterprise with which they sign a contract for their remaining education and likely employment.

Shifting Economic Trends. Since the 2008 publication of the original *Global Developments of Community Colleges, Technical Colleges, and Further Education Programs* (Elsner, Boggs, & Irwin, 2008), community colleges in the United States have received a significant amount of attention. The severe and stubborn economic downturn that had already begun when the book was published provided the incentive for many unemployed and underemployed workers to attend community colleges to pick up the skills they would need to reenter the workforce or to secure better jobs. National news networks and major newspapers in the United States ran stories about the services that community colleges were providing. Families that in better economic times might have sent children to universities instead chose to enroll their children in local community colleges to save money. Community college student enrollment surged, especially during the economic recession from 2007 to 2009. By 2010, the enrollment increases began to moderate as the colleges were forced to cut expenses due to decreases in state financial support.

Increasing College Completion Rates. Another factor that was as important as the effects of the economic downturn in bringing attention to American community colleges was the challenge to increase the college graduation and completion rates of students significantly. On July 14, 2009, President Obama called on American community colleges to increase the number of graduates and program completers by 5 million students over a 10-year period, a 50% increase over the number of graduates and completers in 2008. Although the U.S. Congress was not able to deliver federal funding support to the colleges through the American Graduation Initiative proposed by President Obama, the administration stated its continued commitment to increasing the educational attainment levels of Americans, challenging community colleges to bear a significant part of the burden. On March 30, 2010, at a ceremony at Northern Virginia Community College, President Obama signed H.R. 4872, the Health Care and Education Affordability Reconciliation Act, into law. The act provided $2 billion for the Community College and Career Training Grant Program, a new Trade Adjustment Assistance program focused on workforce preparation.

Debating the Issues—Workforce Preparation vs. Liberal Arts. In both the United States and Canada, there has been some tension between the economic and broader societal roles of the colleges, the latter referring to various college activities that enable people, particularly those facing various disadvantages, to change, improve, and enrich their lives. In the United States, the debate has centered on the value of liberal arts education and how much general education should be required of students in workforce education programs. Understandably, the recent recession has heightened interest in the economic role of the colleges, and in so doing, it has shifted the balance between roles far in the economic direction.

Although in many parts of the world, education is typically a matter of national and social economic progress, in some areas such as French West Africa, there is evidence that education or most precisely the lack of education of youth is increasingly becoming a matter of national security. Because they represent an unproductive influence on the economy, uneducated young people impede social progress. They are also quick to take to the streets to protest the lack of employment opportunities, creating the potential for escalating violence and disruption. Youth can also easily be co-opted by criminals or unsavory politicians who seek to destabilize their own countries. So, revitalizing tertiary education in countries like French West Africa should not be seen as just smart economics; it is increasingly seen as wise politics for any leader seeking stability and wanting to minimize the opportunities for youth to be lost to terrorism or other criminal activities.

Ensuring Productive Long-Term Results. In the United States in 2009, the Bill and Melinda Gates Foundation announced a major post-secondary success initiative with the goal of ensuring that postsecondary education results in a degree or a certificate with genuine economic value. The foundation has set an ambitious goal to double the number of American young people who earn a postsecondary degree or certificate with value in the marketplace by the time they reach age 26. The foundation notes that the types of jobs fueling our economy continue to change rapidly. Success in the workplace demands advanced skills in critical thinking and problem solving, as well as the ability to shift readily from one task or project to another. Workers with strong language and math skills, technological capabilities, and a capacity to work well in teams are most likely to succeed. The U.S. Bureau of Labor Statistics projects that, through 2014, more than half of all new jobs in the United States will require more than a high school diploma. Twenty-two of the fastest-growing career fields will require some postsecondary education. In April 2010, six national community college organizations—representing trustees, administrators, faculty, and students—signed a call to action to commit member institutions to match President Obama's 2020 goal.

Rallying the Call for a National Strategy

Job creation and employment have become significant policy issues in countries throughout the world. Consequently, the postsecondary or tertiary sector of education and training has emerged as a key element in preparing people with the skills they will need for their future careers. The recent global economic recession has taught us how interconnected the world is. And, it has also taught us how important workforce education and training are to economic recovery and development. In this global society and economy, problems are no longer geographically isolated, and educators and policymakers need opportunities to learn from each other. That is the motivation for profiling the global development of community colleges, technical colleges, and further education programs.

References

Biden, J. (2009, July). Keynote address at the UNESCO World Conference on Higher Education, Paris, France. Retrieved from http://www.unesco.org/education/wche/speeches/jill-biden-speech-2009WCHE.pdf

Elsner, P. A. (2015). Preface to Revised Edition. In P. A. Elsner, G. R. Boggs, & J. T. Irwin (Eds.), *Global development of community colleges, technical colleges, and further education programs* (rev. ed., p. XV). Washington, DC: American Association of Community Colleges.

Elsner, P. A., Boggs, G. R., & Irwin, J. T. (Eds.). (2008). *Global development of community colleges, technical colleges, and further education programs*. Washington, DC: American Association of Community Colleges.

Elsner, P. A., Boggs, G. R., & Irwin, J. T. (Eds.). (2015). *Global development of community colleges, technical colleges, and further education programs* (rev. ed.). Washington, DC: American Association of Community Colleges.

Friedman, T. L. (2007). *The world is flat: A brief history of the twenty-first century*. New York, NY: Pixador.

Mellow, G. (2014, December 18). Gainful employment and higher education funding: Investing in programs that work. *Huffington Post*. Retrieved from http://www.huffingtonpost.com/gail-mellow/highered_funding_b_6342866.html

National Center on Education and the Economy. (2008). *Tough choices or tough times: The report of the New Commission on the Skills of the American Workforce*. Retrieved from http://www.skillscommission.org/wp-content/uploads/2010/05/ToughChoices_EXECSUM.pdf

Organisation for Economic Co-operation and Development. (2013). *Education at a glance 2013: OECD indicators*. Paris, France: Author.

Webster, M. (2014, October 29). Could a robot steal your job? *USA Today*, p. 1.

GEORGE R. BOGGS *is president and CEO emeritus of the American Association of Community Colleges and superintendent/president emeritus of Palomar College. He teaches classes in emerging issues in higher education for doctoral programs at San Diego State University and National American University and consults internationally.*

PAUL ELSNER *is chancellor emeritus of the Maricopa Community College District in Arizona. He serves on the board of directors for Sias International University in Zhengzhou, People's Republic of China, and has spoken and consulted in the United Arab Emirates, Qatar, Singapore, China, Australia, New Zealand, Japan, Ireland, England, South Africa, and other countries.*

JUDITH IRWIN *is managing director of Connect Globally. Organizations with whom she has worked include the American International Recruitment Council, the Center for Global Advancement of Community Colleges, the American Association of Community Colleges, and the Business-Higher Education Forum.*

10

This chapter argues that increasing human capital through a combination of university and community college education promotes greater economic growth in developing countries.

Community Colleges, Human Capital, and Economic Growth in Developing Countries

Darryl M. Tyndorf Jr., Chris R. Glass

National policymakers view tertiary education as an essential element for countries to compete in a global knowledge economy (Shrivastava & Shrivastava, 2014). Massification agendas, policies seeking to increase tertiary education enrollments, especially in developing countries, have tended to focus on 4-year tertiary education (Bashir, 2007; Castro, Bernasconi, & Verdisco, 2001; Holmes, 2013; Roggow, 2014; Woods, 2013; Zhang & Hagedorn, 2014), but such a narrow focus artificially limits the propensity for economic growth in developing countries (Wang & Seggie, 2013). Community college education provides an affordable and accessible education (Spangler & Tyler, 2011) and an industry-specific labor force that increases human capital and spurs economic growth (Roggow, 2014).

This chapter argues that increasing human capital through a combination of university and community college education promotes greater economic growth in developing countries. We begin by reviewing how the expansion of community college education provides greater access for students from more diverse socioeconomic backgrounds. We then use a longitudinal analysis of macroeconomic growth from over 150 countries to demonstrate the economic benefits of community college education. We emphasize that community colleges contribute equally to economic growth as traditional 4-year institutions, and there is a comparative advantage for developing countries that expand the community college sector. To maximize the effect of community college education, policymakers must communicate the value of community college education, expand developmental education, and improve metrics for evidence-based decision making.

New Directions for Community Colleges, no. 177, Spring 2017 © 2017 Wiley Periodicals, Inc.
Published online in Wiley Online Library (wileyonlinelibrary.com) • DOI: 10.1002/cc.20246

105

International Adoption of the U.S. Community College Model

Developing countries have found that increasing educational capacity demands partnerships that help students across socioeconomic levels (Altbach, 2013; Bashir, 2007). Educational capacity development initially focused on partnerships with traditional universities (Bashir, 2007; Woods, 2013) because of the prestige associated with university-level degrees (Castro et al., 2001; Roggow, 2014; Wang & Seggie, 2013; Zhang & Hagedorn, 2014). Although 4-year tertiary education provides active research agendas on issues relevant to the respective country, partnerships with traditional 4-year universities do not necessarily provide the accessible and affordable education needed to increase human capital to improve economic growth (Mellow & Katopes, 2009). There is a desperate need for institutions that link education needs with the needs of the market and community (Hewitt & Lee, 2006; Schroeder & Hatton, 2006), and community colleges are the ideal bridge between local communities and the global labor market (Spangler & Tyler, 2011). Community colleges provide this more flexible, short-cycle education focused on immediate workforce training needs (Kintzer & Bryant, 1998; Levin, 2001; UNESCO, 2003; Wang & Seggie, 2013). Without community college education, existing employment opportunities go unmet and additional employment opportunities are not created.

Furthermore, community colleges are experienced with facilitating developmental education. Developing countries have increased enrollments in primary education by at least 20%, which has increased demand for tertiary education. Despite such progress, educational inequality is still evident in developing countries due to lack of accessibility based on disadvantages such as poverty, gender, location, and ethnicity (UNESCO, 2015). In addition, dropout rates in developing countries are such that at least 20% of primary education students will not reach their last grade (UNESCO, 2015). Because of educational inequality and dropout rates, many students in developing countries need developmental education that provides the general knowledge intended to yield economic, social, developmental, or political improvements (Cohen, Brawer, & Kisker, 2014; UNESCO, 2015). Community colleges in developing countries increase human capital by providing developmental education necessary for students to transition directly from high school to skilled employment or a university education (Spangler & Tyler, 2011).

Developing countries have begun to engage the U.S. community college model to complement 4-year university partnership strategies (Cutright, 2014; Kotamraju, 2014; Raby, 2012; Roggow, 2014; UNESCO, 2003; Wang & Seggie, 2013). Table 10.1 is a list of countries engaging a U.S. community college model with many of them contacting Community Colleges for International Development for expertise on establishing or restructuring a community college model to bring affordable, accessible,

Table 10.1   Countries Importing Community College Education

Country	Classification
Aruba	Developing
Brazil	Developing
Chile	Developing
China	Developed
China, Hong Kong Special Administrative Region	Developing
Egypt	Developed
Georgia	Developed
Ghana	Developing
India	Developed
Indonesia	Developed
Japan	Developed
Jordan	Developing
Kuwait	Developed
Malaysia	Developing
Mexico	Developed
Namibia	Developing
Nigeria	Developed
Qatar	Developing
Saudi Arabia	Developing
South Africa	Developed
Trinidad and Tobago	Developing
Tunisia	Developing
Turkey	Developing
Vietnam	Developed
Yemen	Developed

and adaptable curriculum (Cutright, 2014; Hewitt & Lee, 2006; Mellow & Katopes, 2009; Schroeder & Hatton, 2006; Spangler & Tyler, 2011; Wang & Seggie, 2012; Woods, 2013).

Measuring the Economic Benefits of Community College Education

Economists emphasize the role of capital and labor and the factors of production—bound by limited resources—as determinants of *economic growth*, the increase in output of goods and services an economy produces over a period measured by gross domestic product (GDP) (Cortright, 2001; Smith, 1776). Economic thought reflects the belief that knowledge significantly contributes to economic growth because it is nonrival, a good that can be consumed by many at the same time without diminishing the ability of other people to use it, and partly excludable compared to other economic goods, making education an important input for sustainable growth (Cortright, 2001).

The impact of education can be analyzed through microeconomic and macroeconomic analysis. Microeconomics and macroeconomics provide different approaches to measuring the return on education. Microeconomic analysis examines the private or narrow social returns on education (Psacharopoulos & Patrinos, 2004) whereas macroeconomic analysis examines the proximate causes and mechanics of economic growth (Cortright, 2001; Greiner, Semmler, & Gong, 2005; Hartwig, 2014; Romer, 1994). Microeconomic analysis has demonstrated there is a 5 to 15% increase in lifetime wages per year of schooling, with even greater returns for disadvantaged families (Harmon et al., 2003; Psacharopoulos & Patrinos, 2004). However, microeconomic analysis cannot provide insight into the effects of education on economic growth (Cortright, 2001). Macroeconomic analysis has since expanded from engaging the role of capital, labor, and unexplainable technology increases to engaging the spillover effects of education on economic growth. To measure the economic impact of community college education, macroeconomic analyses examine the effects of human capital enhancing policies (Hartwig, 2014; Lucas, 1988; Uzawa, 1965).

Economic Impact of Community Colleges in the Developing World

The measurement of the economic benefits of community college education demonstrates the need for engagement of the community colleges as equal contributors to economic development in developing countries and there is a comparative advantage for developing countries expanding community college education.

Community Colleges as Equal Contributors to Economic Growth in Developing Countries. Our longitudinal analysis of World Bank data (1995–2014) demonstrates that increases in human capital, through a combination of university and community college education, promotes greater economic growth (GDP). Developing countries that have expanded their community college sector experienced a positive and significant effect on economic growth. Moreover, the expansion of community college capacity demonstrated an improvement in economic growth over time and occurred in the medium-term lag on economic growth; thus, the combination of community college and university-level education supported economic growth with initiatives supporting the short-cycle labor force impact of the community college model.

Community colleges have a central role in ensuring developing countries are part of the global knowledge economy. Well-developed community college systems allowed developing countries to respond rapidly to global labor market needs by making education more affordable and accessible for students (Cutright, 2014; Hewitt & Lee, 2006; Mellow & Katopes, 2009; Schroeder & Hatton, 2006; Spangler & Tyler, 2011; Wang & Seggie, 2013; Woods, 2013). Wang and Seggie (2013) found that a narrow focus on a single sector of higher education limits economic growth in developing countries. Community colleges provide a workforce-specific education designed in cooperation with community partners tailored to local needs (Roggow, 2014). The lack of development of the community college section constrains capacity for developing countries to respond to immediate workforce demands and inhibits economic growth (Cohen et al., 2014; Hewitt & Lee, 2006; Wang & Seggie, 2013).

When it comes to sustainable development, developing countries must view community college sector and university sector as complementary approaches to human capital development for economic growth. Unfortunately, countries often pursue strategies that emphasize the pursuit of global rankings and the developing of world-class universities (Bashir, 2007; Roggow, 2014; Wang & Seggie, 2013; Woods, 2013; Zhang & Hagedorn, 2014). Despite the attention and prestige received by a handful of world-class universities, community colleges provide a high rate of return on investment in education, and national policies should concentrate on the development of this sector. In a global knowledge economy, advanced education is no longer a luxury. In a global labor market, community colleges are major players in increasing human capital. Higher education has a role in international development, and the interactions between community college and their local communities are central to human capital development.

Universities, nongovernmental organizations, and governments must recognize the central role that community colleges have as an intermediate option between high school and university-level education; and the entire higher education system must be coordinated such that there are stronger linkages between the K–12, community college, and university sectors of the educational system. However, in general, national policymakers have not fully leveraged community colleges bridge-spanning capacity to expand the capacity of the entire educational system. The diversification of the postsecondary education sector creates a more resilient educational system that allows developing countries to adapt to a rapidly changing global labor.

National strategies that focus on the university sector are less likely to help people recover quickly from social dislocation or economic collapse. This is especially true in developing countries that often have more entrenched issues with stratification by social class (UNESCO, 2015). Community colleges share wealth by increasing human capital of larger more diverse groups of citizens. Expanding community college education not only provides individuals with better standards of living as citizens develop job skills and increase family income, it also raises up the entire society by expanding the middle class. Developing countries must expand the community college sector to increase the number of citizens with a postsecondary education.

Although we are hopeful for the future, we believe that, at this moment, the promise of community colleges' contribution to human capital development remains unfulfilled. Community colleges are the fulcrums that could significantly expand access, increase human capital, and spur economic growth. As open access institutions, they offer a range of technical degrees and provide a pathway to the attainment of university-level degrees for a more diverse demographic of students. As we discuss in the final section of this chapter, national policies aimed at expanding the community college sector are inhibited in part by the lack of metrics to quantify community colleges' contribution to economic growth. When developing countries invest in the community college sector, the result is greater economic growth in addition to the fact that a greater number of citizens have attained higher levels of education.

Comparative Advantages for Developing Countries Expanding Community College Education.   Our research suggests a second, related point: developing countries that import the U.S. community college model have significantly greater economic growth (GDP) compared with developing countries that do not import the U.S. community college model. Community colleges are not just equal contributors to economic growth; they provide developing countries that expand this sector a comparative advantage over developing countries that do not. Because the infrastructure necessary to expand enrollment in the community college sector is less expensive than that of the expensive facilities, equipment, and faculty to invest in world-class universities, investment in the community college sector provides an efficient alternative. Educating a community college student is about one third the cost of educating a 4-year college student— $31,882 vs. $10,481 (Mellow & Katopes, 2009). This is not to suggest that developing countries that invest in world-class research universities do not also enjoy a comparative advantage over those that do not. It does suggest, however, that investment in community college sector is an affordable alternative for developing countries that provides strategic advantages. Investment in multiple community colleges throughout a country creates a more resilient educational system capable of adapting to community needs than narrow investments in a single world-class university.

Our analysis indicates that developing countries that increased tertiary education enrollments by expanding the community college sector attain a 1.0% increase in GDP per capita for each 10% increase in tertiary education enrollment. We recognize that a 10% increase in enrollment is a significant challenge for developing countries; we do not take lightly the significant national investment such an increase necessitates. Furthermore, we recognize that a 10% increase would require a medium- or long-term strategic investment in the community college sector.

Nonetheless, our longitudinal analysis of World Bank data suggest this long-term view, in fact, is what is required. Longitudinal data show that medium-term—10 years or more—investment in community college sector is associated with economic growth, whereas short-term—less than 10 years—is not. In addition, the effects of long-term investment—20 years or more—demonstrates that the economic benefit of investment levels out and no longer provides a comparative advantage. These data suggest that investment in the community college sector is not a quick fix that provides a jolt of economic growth; however, developing countries that have developed medium-term strategies have benefited from sustained investment in this sector although the benefit of that investment levels out after about 20 years.

It is clear that sustained investment to increase tertiary enrollment by expanding the community college sector provides developing countries a comparative advantage of labor by helping to meet workforce demands comparative with developing countries who do not expand tertiary enrollments. We believe the comparative advantage is the direct result from the ability of community colleges to educate citizens from a wider range of socioeconomic backgrounds. Community colleges are critical for developing countries in the early growth stage that provide greater long-run positive economic benefit and help countries provide practical workforce training that readily adapts to the changing conditions in the global economy. Enrollment growth of 10% is not a modest goal; nonetheless, there is a demonstrable benefit to developing countries that invest in community college sector to expand access and increase tertiary education enrollment.

Recommendations

To maximize the effect of community college education, policymakers must communicate the value of the community college to policymakers, expand developmental education, and improve metrics for evidence-based decision making.

Communicating the Value of the Community College to Policymakers. Diversification of the American higher education system—through the expansion the community college system—increased higher education opportunities for most of the American population (Altbach, 2013; Marmolejo, 2012). Community colleges provide immediate and longer term recovery to disaster-stricken communities, education programs linked to the productive sector, and developmental education to university transfer students (Hewitt & Lee, 2006; Mellow & Katopes, 2009; Schroeder & Hatton, 2006). Community colleges are adaptable and responsive to the diverse needs of local populations. They provide an education that develops midlevel managers; delivers paraprofessional, technical, occupational, vocational, and English-language programs; and developmental or transfer education (Raby, 2012). We believe the responsiveness of community colleges to adapt to the communities they serve improves skills and allows developing countries to take advantage of economic opportunities. Community colleges also help people in the workforce adapt to global economic change (Hewitt & Lee, 2006).

Expanding Developmental Education in the Developing World. We believe that community colleges can increase tertiary enrollment by expanding developmental education. Community colleges prepare the workforce by providing basic literacy and mathematics education to highly specialized technical skills tailored to regional business or industry needs. Increased tertiary education demand in developed countries led to the struggle of many students needing developmental education (Cohen et al., 2014). By investing in developmental education, community colleges open pathways for adult learners who were underserved by the primary and secondary education sector. Without the bridge that developmental education can provide, these citizens would be left behind. As demand for tertiary education increases, developmental education is no longer an optional component of the community college sector. It must be a central aspect of massification and diversification of tertiary education policy initiatives in developing countries.

Improving Metrics for Evidence-Based Decision Making for Partnerships. UNESCO relies on individual countries to supply higher education data based on the International Standard Classification of Education (ISCED). UNESCO's Institute for Statistics works closely with countries and data collection agencies to ensure mappings are in accordance with standards. The ISCED level 5 association with community colleges may not represent all the education curricula offered at the community college. Data collection does not provide transnational education initiatives. Scarce data on transnational education limits the ability to understand the impact of such initiatives. In hopes of understanding the impact transnational education of community college have in developing countries, data need to be gathered on the type of transnational initiative, the strategic initiatives and the respective measurements, and the quantitative and qualitative outcome of the transnational initiative.

References

Altbach, P. G. (2013). *Global perspectives on higher education: The international imperative in higher education.* Rotterdam, The Netherlands: Sense Publishers.

Bashir, S. (2007). *Trends in international trade in higher education: Implications and options for developing countries* (Education: Working Paper Series, 6). Washington, DC: World Bank.

Castro, C. M., Bernasconi, A., & Verdisco, A. (2001). *Community colleges: Is there a lesson in them for Latin America?* (Sustainable Development Department Technical Paper Series). Washington, DC: Inter-American Development Bank.

Cohen, A. M., Brawer, F. B., & Kisker, C. B. (2014). *The American community college* (6th ed.). San Francisco, CA: Jossey-Bass.

Cortright, J. (2001). New growth theory, technology and learning: A practitioner's guide. *Reviews of Economic Development Literature and Practice, 4*(6), 1–32.

Cutright, M. (2014). Meeting emergent needs in Uganda: A path to accelerated development of community and work colleges. *Community College Journal of Research and Practice, 38*(8), 733–739, doi:10.1080/10668926.2014.89708

Greiner, A., Semmler, W., & Gong, G. (2005). *Economic growth: A time series perspective.* Princeton, NJ: Princeton University Press.

Harmon, C., Oosterbeek, H., & Walker, I. (2003). The returns to education: Microeconomics. *Journal of Economic Surveys, 17*(2), 115–155. doi:10.1111/1467-6419.00191

Hartwig, J. (2014). Testing the Uzawa-Lucas model with OECD data. *Research in Economics, 68*(2), 144–156. doi:10.1016/j.rie.2014.01.002

Hewitt, M. J., & Lee, K. (2006). Community college for international development. *Community College Journal, 76*(3), 46–49.

Kintzer, F. C., & Bryant, D. W. (1998). Global perceptions of the community college. *Community College Review, 26*(3), 35–55.

Kotamraju, P. (2014). The Indian vocational education and training (VET) system: Status, challenges, and options. *Community College Journal of Research and Practice, 38*(8), 740–747. doi:10.1080/10668926.2014.897085

Levin, J. S. (2001). *Globalizing the community college: Strategies for change in the twenty-first century.* New York, NY: Palgrave.

Lucas, R. E. (1988). On the mechanics of economic development. *Journal of Monetary Economics, 22*(1), 3–42.

Marmolejo, F. (2012). *Global engagement at US community colleges: International briefs for higher education leaders.* Washington, DC: American Council on Education.

Mellow, G. O., & Katopes, P. (2009). A prescription for the emerging world: The global potential of the community college model. *Change: The Magazine of Higher Learning, 41*(5), 55–59. http://doi.org/10.3200/CHNG.41.5.55-61

Psacharopoulos, G., & Patrinos, H. A. (2004). Human capital and rates of return. In G. Johnes & J. Johnes (Eds.), *International handbook on the economics of education* (pp. 1–57). Cheltenham, UK: Edward Elgar Publishing Limited.

Raby, R. L. (2012). *Global engagement at US community colleges: International briefs for higher education leaders.* Washington, DC: American Council on Education.

Roggow, M. J. (2014). The vulnerability of China's vocational colleges: How the global economy is impacting vocational colleges in China. *Community College Journal of Research and Practice, 38*(8), 748–754. doi:10.1080/10668926.2014.897086

Romer, P. M. (1994). The origins of endogenous growth. *Journal of Economic Perspectives, 8*(1), 3–22.

Schroeder, K., & Hatton, M. (2006). Community colleges: Untapped assistance for international disaster relief. *Community College Journal, 76*(7), 48–53.

Shrivastava, M., & Shrivastava, S. (2014). Political economy of higher education: Comparing South Africa to trends in the world. *Higher Education, 67*(6), 809–822. doi:10.1007/s10734-013-9709-6

Smith, A. (1776). *Wealth of nations.* Amherst, NY: Prometheus Books.

Spangler, M. S., & Tyler, A. Q. (2011). Identifying fit of mission and environment: Applying the American community college model internationally. In J. E. Lane & K. Kinser (Eds.), *New Directions for Higher Education: No. 155, Multinational colleges and universities: Leading, governing, and managing international branch campuses* (pp. 41–52). San Francisco, CA: Jossey-Bass. doi:10.1002/he.443

UNESCO. (2003). *Globalization and higher education: The implications for north-south dialogue.* Retrieved from: http://www.unesco.org/education/studyingabroad/highlights/global_forum/gf_oslo_may03.shtml

UNESCO. (2015). *Education for all 2000–2015: Achievements and challenges.* EFA Global Monitoring Report.

Uzawa, H. (1965). Optimum technical change in an aggregate model of economic growth. *International Economic Review, 6*(1), 18–31.

Wang, W., & Seggie, F. N. (2013). Different missions of community college systems in two different countries: Community education in Taiwan versus vocational education in Turkey. *Community College Journal of Research and Practice, 37*(1), 18–36. doi:10.1080/10668920903213198

Woods, B. (2013). Going global: Community colleges are developing international programs to prepare students for global opportunities and to expand their education model to other parts of the world. *Community College Journal, 48*(1), 32–38.

Zhang, Y. L., & Hagedorn, L. S. (2014). Chinese education agents views of American community colleges. *Community College Journal of Research and Practice, 38*(8), 721–732. doi:10.1080/10668926.2014.897082

DARRYL M. TYNDORF JR. *is a senior lecturer for Doctor of Education in the School of Education at Aurora University and adjuncts for economics and political science at various institutions.*

CHRIS R. GLASS *is the program coordinator for Old Dominion University's doctoral program in Community College Leadership.*

INDEX

NEW DIRECTIONS FOR COMMUNITY COLLEGE

ORDER FORM SUBSCRIPTION AND SINGLE ISSUES

DISCOUNTED BACK ISSUES:

Use this form to receive 20% off all back issues of *New Directions for Community College*.
All single issues priced at **$23.20** (normally $29.00)

TITLE	ISSUE NO.	ISBN
_____	_____	_____
_____	_____	_____
_____	_____	_____

Call 1-800-835-6770 or see mailing instructions below. When calling, mention the promotional code JBNND to receive your discount. For a complete list of issues, please visit www.wiley.com/WileyCDA/WileyTitle/productCd-CC.html

SUBSCRIPTIONS: (1 YEAR, 4 ISSUES)

☐ New Order   ☐ Renewal

U.S.	☐ Individual: $89	☐ Institutional: $356
CANADA/MEXICO	☐ Individual: $89	☐ Institutional: $398
ALL OTHERS	☐ Individual: $113	☐ Institutional: $434

Call 1-800-835-6770 or see mailing and pricing instructions below.
Online subscriptions are available at www.onlinelibrary.wiley.com

ORDER TOTALS:

Issue / Subscription Amount: $ _____

Shipping Amount: $ _____
(for single issues only – subscription prices include shipping)

Total Amount: $ _____

SHIPPING CHARGES:

First Item $6.00
Each Add'l Item $2.00

(No sales tax for U.S. subscriptions. Canadian residents, add GST for subscription orders. Individual rate subscriptions must be paid by personal check or credit card. Individual rate subscriptions may not be resold as library copies.)

BILLING & SHIPPING INFORMATION:

☐ **PAYMENT ENCLOSED:** *(U.S. check or money order only. All payments must be in U.S. dollars.)*

☐ **CREDIT CARD:**   ☐ VISA   ☐ MC   ☐ AMEX

Card number _____ Exp. Date_____

Card Holder Name_____ Card Issue # _____

Signature _____ Day Phone_____

☐ **BILL ME:** *(U.S. institutional orders only. Purchase order required.)*

Purchase order # _____
Federal Tax ID 13559302 • GST 89102-8052

Name_____

Address_____

Phone_____ E-mail_____

Copy or detach page and send to: **John Wiley & Sons, Inc. / Jossey Bass**
PO Box 55381
Boston, MA 02205-9850

PROMO JBNND